NLP
for ROOKIES

Titles in the *for* ROOKIES series

About the authors

Becky Mallery is a psychologist, coach and NLP Master Practitioner. She trained in NLP with Richard Bandler, John La Valle, Michael Neill and Paul McKenna. She also assisted Paul McKenna on his London seminars. Becky is completing an MSc in Applied Positive Psychology at the University of East London. Using her NLP and psychology knowledge, she founded the business StrengthsWork, coaching individuals in areas such as resilience to help manage stress, building on personal strengths and increasing confidence. She currently gives visiting lectures on positive psychology to universities, with recent presentations on emotional intelligence. Becky is a graduate member of the British Psychological Society and of their Special Group in Coaching Psychology.

Katherine Russell was trained in NLP by Richard Bandler, John La Valle and Paul McKenna. She is an NLP Master Practitioner, advanced hypnotherapist, corporate trainer, coach and personal therapist. Her experience includes: developing and presenting corporate training; giving visiting lectures to schools, corporations and local interest groups; assisting on McKenna training programmes; volunteer work with Marie Curie Cancer Care; and running her own private practice, i2iTherapies (i2itherapies. com), which specializes in one-to-one coaching, counselling and hypnotherapy for conditions such as depression, fears and phobias, and stopping smoking.

NLP
for ROOKIES

Copyright © 2009 LID Editorial Empresarial and Marshall Cavendish Limited

First published in 2009 by

Marshall Cavendish Limited
Fifth Floor
32–38 Saffron Hill
London EC1N 8FH
United Kingdom
T: +44 (0)20 7421 8120
F: +44 (0)20 7421 8121
sales@marshallcavendish.co.uk
www.marshallcavendish.co.uk

A member of **BPR**

businesspublishersroundtable.com

Marshall Cavendish is a trademark of Times Publishing Limited

Other Marshall Cavendish offices: Marshall Cavendish International (Asia) Private
Limited, 1 New Industrial Road, Singapore 536196 • Marshall Cavendish Corporation.
99 White Plains Road, Tarrytown NY 10591–9001, USA • Marshall Cavendish International
(Thailand) Co Ltd. 253 Asoke, 12th Floor, Sukhumvit 21 Road, Klongtoey Nua, Wattana,
Bangkok 10110, Thailand • Marshall Cavendish (Malaysia) Sdn Bhd, Times Subang, Lot 46,
Subang Hi-Tech Industrial Park, Batu Tiga, 40000 Shah Alam, Selangor Darul Ehsan,
Malaysia

A CIP record for this book is available from the British Library

ISBN 978-0-462-09958-3

Illustrations by Nuria Aparicio and Joan Guardiet

Printed and bound in Great Britain by
TJ International Limited, Padstow, Cornwall

Contents

PNL   NLP

Introduction

What is NLP?

NLP stands for "Neuro Linguistic Programming", which is a methodology designed to study, model and train individuals in human excellence.

- **Neuro** = neurological; that is, to do with the mind, its thinking and the nervous system.
- **Linguistic** = language and communication; that is, their use, the understanding and the influence of words both internally and externally.
- **Programming** = the structures, processes and habits running our behaviour.

Another way of describing NLP is as your own personal toolbox for accessing and influencing the human mind.

Imagine the infinite possibilities available to you if you chose to learn the techniques that would enable you to copy the inspiring presentation skills of your manager, train you to recreate the imagination and drive of your CEO, and teach you how to develop similar skills to that of a top salesperson.

Through NLP you can fully understand how the human mind works, what determines its thinking and behaviour, and how you can learn to influence it.

Learn how other people organize their thoughts and feelings to produce the results they do. Understand the motivation, strategies and programming behind human behaviour, and obtain the skills necessary to allow you to recognize, model and recreate the techniques that will deliver all the options and outcomes of your desire and choosing.

A brief history

Created back in the 1970s by the curious and questioning minds of Dr Richard Bandler (then a student psychologist at the University of California, Santa Cruz) and John Grinder (an assistant linguistics professor), NLP's original purpose was to provide an answer to these simple questions:

* How is it some people excel at certain things, when others do not?
* What makes them different and what is it that they are doing differently?

To begin answering this, Bandler and Grinder fused their already extensive knowledge and began developing a methodology that would study the "language of change". They focused on three unique individuals: Fritz Perls, a psychotherapist and founder of the Gestalt School of Therapy, Virginia Satir, a talented family therapist, and Milton Erickson, a world famous psychologist and hypnotherapist.

At that time, each of the three therapists was considered a genius within their own chosen field of Change Therapy, and all retained a common theme that set them apart from their peers, in that they were all well known for being able to establish change within even the most difficult of patients, creating successful cases where other therapists had failed.

Bandler and Grinder observed, recorded and modelled the work of this magical trio and, by carefully studying their specific use of language, behavioural thought processes and actions, the two researchers identified certain patterns and structures, that, once copied, would allow other individuals to produce similar astounding results (a process that would later be known as "modelling human excellence"). These findings were then compiled and delivered through Bandler's Master's thesis and later published as *The Structure of Magic*.

The foundations for a whole new school of therapy were now in place, and the methodology that is now known as neuro linguistic programming came unintentionally into creation.

As with many things, NLP has subsequently undergone its own natural evolution and is now trained, studied and used the world over. Countless books have been written on the subject; institutions have been established; further techniques, theories and structures are continuously identified and developed; and today NLP is recognized as one of the most effective and influential tools used in personal, social and corporate contexts.

How can NLP benefit you?

The world today is dramatically and constantly changing, with individual, client and management expectations operating at a very high level, and tolerance for failure at an all-time low.

If you want to survive, cope and excel in today's corporate environment, then you must be prepared to continuously develop certain skills and maintain constant behavioural flexibility. NLP can teach you to understand why, when and how to go about achieving this.

Soft skills are becoming an ever more essential

4 ingredient in today's market, and the old cliché, "people buy people", has never been truer.

People don't like to be sold to, they like to buy, and in this book not only are we going to teach you how to have individuals buying into you, but also you are going to learn how to improve your overall performance within every function and aspect of your life.

As you journey through this book, we are going to introduce you to the specific NLP techniques that will teach you how to obtain the excellence that you desire and need for:

- Confidence, motivation and inspiration.
- Meetings and interviews.
- Competing for advancement in your career.
- Winning and closing deals.
- Time and people management.
- Presentation skills that have clarity and impact.

By understanding the thinking behind all behaviour, you will gain insight into how your beliefs, values, habitual structures and perception of life can have positive or negative influences upon how you choose to interact with the world, and the effect you have on it and it has on you.

It is not life itself that limits us, but rather our own limited beliefs, expectations and perceptions of the choices that are available to us.

Notes

We rely upon our minds to provide us with everything we need to survive, function and interact with the world and life in general. The mind provides us with an identity and a belief system; it creates our dreams and our values, learns the necessary skills and gives us the understanding that supplies our lives with existence and meaning. In this chapter we will learn how our mind is structured, how we process thought, create our habits and perceive the world around us. We will learn how to look upon life in a way that unlocks our choices and gains us access to the power of our own creativity.

CHAPTER 1

The limitless potential of your mind

Perceptions

We are all a part of the same world, breathing in the same air and standing under the same blue sky, but our individual experience and understanding of this world is as unique to us as our fingerprints.

We all view reality very differently. Two people can sit in exactly the same room, can be a part of exactly the same business meeting and be presented with exactly the same information, but neither will ever be able to give exactly the same account of that meeting if questioned about its contents later. And interestingly, although both accounts are different, they will still in their own unique way be completely true.

This is because, despite the fact that both individuals have sat side by side in the same meeting, their individual perceptions of the discussed agenda, the speaker and the issues raised, as well as their personal judgements, will still end up being completely different.

During that meeting, although both people will have observed exactly the same presentation, it will have been observed through different realities, resulting in different concluding interpretations, in

8 which the speaker's intended message may or may not have been fully understood.

Imagine how many arguments are caused and deals lost because of a simple misunderstanding or a miscommunication of information. No two people are ever looking at the world from the same point of view. There is no such thing as reality, only our perception of it.

Rookie Buster

There is no such thing as reality, only our perception of it.

The reason why the police are always keen to try and get as many witnesses as possible to come forward after a crime has been committed is because one witness statement is unfortunately not enough. Evidence based upon the opinion of one person alone will only highlight one singular viewpoint, influenced by that person's individual understanding of events, and therefore cannot account for all the other valuable information that was potentially available at the time.

Perception is like a Rubik's cube

If we were to view just one side of the Rubik's cube, we would observe only one colour – for example, green. On that knowledge alone, we could then assume that the entire Rubik's cube was in fact green, and even go as far as to argue to others that this was the case, based on our current understanding.

However, should someone then come and turn our Rubik's cube over, we would notice that it now presented a completely different side with a different colour – yellow, say. Based upon this new understanding, should we now conclude that the entire Rubik's cube has become yellow, or has it become yellow and green?

We could accept the new judgement, or we could then decide to go one step further and choose instead to look at the Rubik's cube from every possible angle, becoming aware that actually this cube has sides of many different colours, including blue, white, orange and red.

Our originally perceived green coloured cube has suddenly evolved into a multi-coloured cube, and what's more, it can be evolved even further should we ask the magical question "What if?"

What if we then chose to spend some time twisting and turning the Rubik's cube's various layers into different directions, and did this until all the individual, tiny coloured squares were mixed up together and no side displayed just one colour – what could we then learn and what would our conclusion be?

Just this: nothing can be fully understood by one viewpoint alone. And from this springs another lesson: every problem has a solution; it may sometimes just need another perspective.

Rookie Buster

Every problem has a solution; it may sometimes just need another perspective.

Maps

In NLP we use the analogy of "maps" to describe the neurological blueprint that we each work with when attempting to understand and decode our personal experience of the world around us.

The "map" is simply our interpretation of our own reality, our past, present and future. It is constructed through our learned lessons and behaviours, our beliefs, values, identity and interpretations of objects, sounds, tastes, smells, feelings, people and events. Each and every single element of all of our experiences is broken down, recoded, recreated and stored within our mind as a neurological map. This map is an intricately detailed blueprint for our subconscious mind to follow, to refer back to and to utilize in our translations, judgements and

10 understandings of how to appropriately relate and interact with our surrounding environment.

Our maps are predominantly influenced by our perceptions of life and are created as a result of our past understanding. The perceptions we have create a major directional influence upon all of our interpretations of the world, and can alter the way we in which we view life's opportunities and our available choices. But the map is not the territory.

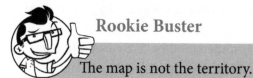

Rookie Buster

The map is not the territory.

How your mind works

Have you ever noticed yourself behaving in a way that you wished you could change, and subsequently found yourself arguing and reasoning with that internal voice inside your head?

Have you ever begun shaking like a leaf the moment you started to contemplate giving an office presentation, even though you know your subject matter inside out, much better than anyone else does?

We can all sometimes behave in a way that we would consciously prefer not to, and consequently we can be left regretting or resenting some of our actions – even occasionally our lack of them.

Rookie Buster

We can all sometimes behave in a way that we would consciously prefer not to.

However, if you are finding you are experiencing and responding to the world in a way that you wished was different, it is important for you now to recognize that these unwanted perceptions and behaviours are not always entirely your fault, or not consciously anyway.

The driving forces behind all our various behaviours begin within structures that are so deeply rooted and complex that if we attempt to control them with conscious and analytical thought alone, we will often struggle to have any influential impact upon them at all. Every action we perform is a response to a combination of various different thoughts, programming, systems, structures, patterns and conditioned understanding. All of our behaviours are a result of more than just one, singular conscious idea, making it very difficult to influence them through logical thought and reasoning alone.

Our minds function on two separate levels:

The conscious mind (logical thinking)

and

The subconscious mind (automatic functioning).

Our *conscious mind* processes all of our logical thought and analytical reasoning. Our conscious mind is the part of our mind that is constantly alert and aware, making value judgements and assessments and arriving at inevitable conclusions. We use our conscious mind to perceive our reality of the world and provide the meaning to all of our experiences, thoughts and actions in a way that can we can understand, recreate and compartmentalize.

Rookie Buster

Our conscious mind is the part of our mind that is constantly alert and aware.

Your conscious mind will be used for, among other things, dates of meetings, colleagues' names and company statistics.

Our *subconscious mind* (or unconscious mind) is the part of our brain that runs all our automatic functions. It operates all of our behavioural strategies, habitual patterns, emotions and memories. Everything that our subconscious mind does is based upon systematic structures, sequences and linked understanding. It is governed by our beliefs, values, identity and expectations, and is constantly seeking out new ways of evolving its systems and streamlining its processes towards efficiency.

Rookie Buster

Our subconscious mind is the part of our brain that runs all our automatic functions. It operates all of our behavioural strategies, habitual patterns, emotions and memories.

Your subconscious mind is used for, among other things, getting to work, operating computer systems, typing emails and making the morning coffee.

Did you know that the subconscious mind actually has no analytical abilities whatsoever? It does not have the logic to decide between right and wrong, or positive and negative.

To understand even negative information, our subconscious must first turn it into a positive, which means every program our subconscious mind is operating has a positive intent driving it. Every bad habit we now have has been originally created for a very good reason… and that includes biting your nails!

The conscious mind

Your conscious mind is the part of your brain that is aware of reading and understanding this statement right now.

Logical and analytical, our conscious mind can be recognized as the thoughts going on within our head, as we perceive and interact with our surrounding world. It's the part of our mind that we use to analyse company statistics or debate the choice, colour and impact of a colleague's tie.

Our internal and external environment is so incredibly detailed and complex that our mind has to operate on a multitude of levels in order to constantly manage this fluctuating information effectively. By processing our information in this way, we become free to manoeuvre through the daily process that is our lives, reacting and adapting to all its experiences.

There are in fact approximately 4 billion pieces of separate information bombarding our senses every single second, and out of all this intricate data our mind must select the elements deemed relevant to us so that they can be processed and responded to accordingly.

To handle this constant level of input, your mind processes most of this information in such a way as to leave your conscious mind aware of only a tiny proportion of it, and free to interact and analyse our daily events. (See also Chapter 3 on the senses.)

For example, in this moment you are able to read this book, debate and reason its content, and at the same time still function on many other levels. You heart is beating, your lungs are breathing, maybe you are holding your body posture upright, while your eyes automatically scan across the pages, your fingers automatically knowing when to turn each page; and at the same time your subconscious is probably keeping a quiet track of the time, the jobs you still have left to do by the end of the day, and the millions of other functions that are simply overlooked by your conscious awareness until we mentioned a couple of them, just then.

In fact, according to the theory of American psychologist George Miller, "The magic number seven, plus or minus two", the conscious mind is only able to keep track of five, seven or nine pieces of

14 information at any given time. This information is not size specific, and can be anything from the thoughts within your head or your awareness of your external environment.

Focus your attention on your surrounding environment right now, and start to notice all the different noises you are beginning to hear going on in the background.

What sounds are you now aware of? Are there any new noises that maybe you hadn't heard or noticed earlier?

The subconscious mind

Not unlike a computer, your subconscious mind operates all of its functions through a series of pre-programmed systematic processes. Every action, gesture, facial expression, movement or habit you now perform is the result of a previously learned and perfected behavioural response.

Think back to your early days at school. Remember how much time you spent sitting at your writing desk, carefully copying down the large letters off the board and on to the page, learning and understanding the meaning behind every single word, the shapes and sound of the letters. How many times did you practise over the years, expanding upon your knowledge, repeating the processes of writing, reading and spelling time and again until eventually you mastered the art of basic reading and writing?

Now think about how many times you've probably jotted down thoughts and ideas, probably taken countless memos, ploughed through numerous reports, and all without a second's conscious thought.

You don't now look at the words on this page

and debate the meaning of every single letter and phrase: instead you automatically read the words and immediately understand their meanings. This is because the processes of reading and writing have now become a perfectly formed subconscious program and habit, driven by an intent (understanding) and formed through combinations of various patterned structures. These structures are neurological thinking (sentence structure, phonetics) and physiological, motor responses (holding a pen or a book). In fact it would be almost impossible for you to look at the words on this page and not understand what they mean.

Through a process of trial and error the subconscious mind lays the foundations for all our future movements, understandings and gestures. Over time your subconscious mind will gradually expand upon them, condense them down and then overgeneralize these patterns, meanings and purposes, so we can seamlessly function through every element of our lives, leaving our conscious mind free to debate the meaning of life and our next pay cheque.

Rookie Buster

Through a process of trial and error the subconscious mind lays the foundations for all our future movements, understandings and gestures.

Programs of behaviour

Before our subconscious mind attempts to learn any new behaviour, it must first perceive an intent for doing so, a reason "why".

When we originally learned "how" to open a door for the very first time, the original intent ("why") instigating the processes may have been anything from "freedom" to "independence" or "attainment". It may have been "freedom" because as a child we may have wanted to

16 open and escape from all closed rooms, or "independence" because we wanted to choose where we could go and when, or it may have been for reasons of "attainment" because there was something shiny and very interesting that we wanted and that was kept behind a cupboard door.

Whatever the original, driving intent, it will have been motivating enough for our mind to begin the processes of learning, applying hours of conscious of trial and error, understanding all the tiny elements and processes involved (cognitive and motor skills – that is, moving our fingers, clutching the handle, contracting our muscles, and so on) until eventually our conscious mind finally understood "how".

Once this "how" was achieved, this new process would have been repeated again and again until eventually our mind had patterned, sequenced and understood it enough to turn it over to our subconscious mind and subsequently for it to become a behavioural program, to be run whenever a combination of intent (why) and a door handle (how) is perceived. But before our subconscious mind attempts to learn any new behaviour, it must first perceive an intent for doing so, a reason "why".

Rookie Buster

Before our subconscious mind attempts to learn any new behaviour, it must first perceive an intent for doing so, a reason "why".

It's all in the learning 17

In NLP, the process of learning can be explained in four stages:

1. Unconscious incompetence
Our mind is completely unaware that there is something it may want to do but currently cannot do. *We are unaware of the door's existence, its function and its potential impact on our lives.*

2. Conscious incompetence
Our mind is aware that there is something we want to do (intent/why) but doesn't yet know how to go about achieving it. *We are aware of the door's impact and we want to know how to open it, but haven't yet figured out how to go about doing so.*

3. Conscious competence
Our mind is aware of "how" we can achieve what it is we want, but it still has to stay focused upon the process in order to achieve it. *We have now worked out how to open the door and have identified all the processes involved to facilitate achieving this, but we still have to focus and think consciously about every element of it.*

4. Unconscious competence
Our mind understands the process and has turned it over to the subconscious mind to become a habitual program, to be run automatically without any conscious thought or awareness. *We are now able to open a door at any time we perceive one and have intent for doing so; we don't have to think consciously about it, our subconscious mind just runs the program automatically.*

Exercise: Never too old to learn new tricks

Read through this exercise, take a piece of paper, and write down the answers to the following questions:

18   **1. If you were to think of something now that you really want to learn, what is it?**
Maybe it's how to give great presentations, acquire confident interview techniques or play golf. *This stage is taking an idea out of unconscious incompetence and bringing it into conscious incompetence.*

2. What is the intent and what are you going to gain?
Create the intent, the "why" for your subconscious. "Why" do you want to learn this? *This stage is taking the steps towards conscious incompetence.*

3. What do you need to do to start learning "how" to do this?
What are the steps you need to put into action? How are you going to begin learning this new program? *At this stage you turn your new program into conscious competence.*

4. What do you need to do to make this program second nature?
How many times a week are you going to practise this new program? How will you recognize you have got there? What will you be doing, and how will you be doing it?

What will you feel, see and hear when you have finally made this new program an unconscious habit? How will it affect your life and what difference will it make?

This is the practice stage – the more you practise something, the better you will become.

This leads to unconscious competence.

Coach's notes

Changing perspectives

We can all experience situations within our lives that would benefit from a simple shift in our perceptions at the time.

1. Think of a recent situation where you have perhaps experienced conflict with another person, or felt overwhelmed by a potential decision or unsettled by the thought of impending circumstances.

2. While you are thinking about the situation, become aware of all the different elements that concern you, or that you don't like or understand, or want to change. Has someone maybe responded in a way you hadn't expected? Are you worried your decision may turn out to be the wrong one? Is there something about a particular situation that is making you uncomfortable?

   If you are struggling to hold all of these thoughts in your mind, write them all down on a piece of paper.

3. Now think about how you would like your situation to resolve. What would be your desired outcome, and what would you like to achieve?

4. With this outcome in mind, now think again about your particular concerns about your situation. Now imagine shifting your current perspective on them so that you alter your viewpoint from being negative to positive (in other words, from seeing the glass as half empty to seeing it as half full).

   What can you gain? How can you use the information you have to achieve your outcome? What will you learn? What opportunities can you now perceive? Who will benefit?

For example:

Why is someone responding in the way that they are? Imagine looking at the situation from their point of view. Could they simply have misinterpreted your words or actions? What are they trying to achieve? How could you positively alter your response to lead both of you towards your goal?

Think about all of the positive outcomes to your possible decision. What could you gain? How will you or others benefit? What could you do instead, and what would make you happy?

Is there something about this situation you can learn from? How can it positively influence your life? Is it something you can positively accept, and if not, will you choose to change it? What other alternatives or opportunities are out there, that you may have simply overlooked?

Remember – there is no such thing as reality, only our perception of it.

Go for it! Whether you have a difficult client, an unsuitable product or a conflict of opinion, the chances are, you are probably only perceiving the problem from one perspective and from one point of view. Occasionally choose to step out of your comfort zone, dare to ask the question "What if?" and then tilt your angle of perception. What new opportunities await you, when you actively choose to look for them?

22 Notes

Notes

In this chapter we will learn the importance of having goals and how to map our way towards attaining them. A company can only exist because it operates on an idea or mission statement which expresses its purpose, and we as individuals are the same. Without clearly defined goals, however, we can sometimes fail to understand the active steps we need to take in order to make our ambitions come true.

CHAPTER 2

What do you really want?

The importance of having goals

All new companies start off with a business plan, a blueprint highlighting all the aspects of the company's targets for the future business year. This detailed map provides the company with all the essential information it needs to begin achieving success.

A business plan contains:
- Company objectives.
- Direction.
- Route on how to get there.
- Details of the tools that are going to be needed.
- What to expect at certain points along the way.
- How and when to assess these objectives and recognize that they have been finally achieved.

Without a perceived destination, a company has no focus or direction, and will struggle to make any progress, let alone operate successfully. To hit a target you must first know where to aim. Your subconscious mind works in exactly the same way. To achieve anything you want to

26   in life, you must first work out what it is you actually want.

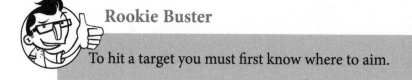

Rookie Buster

To hit a target you must first know where to aim.

In NLP terms, this is known as "well-formedness", or well-formed outcomes.

Now answer these questions:
1. What are your goals?
2. What are you hoping to achieve by reading this book?
3. What is it you want to change or gain?

Our clever subconscious mind has all the tools, adaptability and learning power necessary to deliver us all the goals of our desires, whether it is in our working, social or personal life. One of the main problems we struggle with that prevents us from achieving this, is that we often don't actually know what it is that we want.

Negative or positive

We all have a list of the things we don't want in life and spend an awful lot of time and energy trying to avoid these negatives:
- Don't want to be in debt.
- Don't want to fail the interview.
- Don't want to be rejected.

Unfortunately this is where we let ourselves down and make one of our biggest mistakes.

Remember, our subconscious cannot operate in the negative. Every program and response it operates is always done with a positive intention. It has no logical reasoning and cannot process negative language,

so when our subconscious receives a negative command such as "I 27
don't want to be in debt," it won't understand the "don't" part and will
instead process "I *want* to be in debt."

So "I don't want to fail the interview" becomes "I *want* to fail the
interview," and "I don't want to be rejected" becomes "I *want* to be
rejected."

Remember, our conscious mind can only focus upon a limited
amount of information at any given time (five, seven or nine pieces),
so if we are using this limited amount of attention space to focus only
upon the things we *don't* want to happen, the only reality your conscious mind is perceiving is a negative one.

Rookie Buster

Our conscious mind can only focus upon a limited
amount of information at any given time (five, seven or
nine pieces).

Ironically, because our subconscious mind can only process positive commands, if we focus all of our attention upon things we are
actually trying to avoid, our subconscious is inevitably turning it into
our reality.

You have to maintain your focus upon something in order to know
when to avoid it, which is a great strategy if you want to avoid disappearing down a pothole or standing in something you shouldn't.
However, when it comes to understanding your mind's interpretation
of your own reality, should you choose to spend all of your limited
focus and energy trying to avoid the things you *don't* want in life, you
could end up overlooking and missing the things you *do* want.

From an NLP perspective, to enable any changes to take place, a
goal must first be established.

Once the subconscious mind has an objective in place, it can then
begin developing all the programs necessary (a map) to get there.

28   At this point, write a list of all the things you would do if you knew you could never fail. Next imagine yourself as a company. What is your own business plan for the future?

You can learn to achieve anything you want to in life. What is it that *you* want?

Exercise: Creating our targets

1. Is your goal in the positive?

- What do you actually want? Remember, your subconscious cannot function in the negative, so it is important that you stop focusing upon what you don't want to achieve. *I don't want to fail my interview, I don't want to be disorganized, I don't want to make a fool of myself.*
- Make sure you state your goal as a positive command. What specifically do you want to achieve? What's the benefit, the something to be gained rather than avoided? I want to be successful and professional in my interview, I want to be organized and focused, I want to be confident and relaxed in my interview.

2. Are you doing it for yourself, and is it within your control?

- Are your intentions solely for your own gain, or are you trying to keep someone else happy?
- Does the goal's outcome rely upon others or you?

3. How will you know when you are starting or close to achieving it?

- How will you recognize you are achieving your outcome?
- What will be you be doing when you get it?
- What will you hear, see, and feel?
- What impact will it have on your life, and what will it affect?

4. Is the context of your goal clearly defined?

- What are the specific details of your goal? Clarify what you want and what you don't want.

- When, where, how and with whom do you want it?

Having a clear idea of all the specific elements of your goal will help break down the steps needed to take you there. Chunk down the information into manageable and achievable pieces.

5. What resources do you need to make this happen?

- Do you have the necessary tool or skills to make your goal happen?
- Do you already have the resources, and if not what do you have to do to get them?
- Have you ever done anything like this before, or has anyone else achieved this before, and how can that help you?
- What impact would it make if you acted as though you already had the resources?

6. Is it ecological?

- If you achieve this goal, how will it impact on your life?
- Is it in harmony with all aspects of your life?
- Why do you really want this?
- What will happen if you get it?
- What won't happen if you get it?
- What will happen if you don't get it?
- What won't happen if you don't get it?

7. Have you identified the first steps you need to take?

- What is the very first thing you need to do to start making this goal happen?
- What are your first steps, leading you to take action?
- When are you going to do it?

Only you have the power to make your dreams come true: unless you take the first steps, your ambitions will always remain just wishful thinking.

30

Rookie Buster

Only you have the power to make your dreams come true.

Turning your expectation into reality

For our brain to understand any information, it must recreate the thought within our mind (via our five senses), compare it against our past experiences and understanding, and then have an emotional response to it.

Your mind hates not knowing how to do something. A lot of our fears, insecurities and uncomfortable sensations occur when we are faced with a situation that we have no current examples or references to compare them against.

Remember how nervous you felt on your first day of school, or at your first interview, or meeting someone new for the first time?

We hate not knowing and despise not understanding.

Rookie Buster

We hate not knowing and despise not understanding.

To manage all of the various functions that we have on a daily basis, your subconscious has created various programs of automatic behaviour that run like clockwork. To understand which programs to use, and when and how, your subconscious mind follows an internal map. This map is a creation of our belief systems, values, ideals, identity, past experiences and understanding, our environment, our ambitions 31 and our goals. It's a complete instruction manual to our psyche.

Imagine reading down a menu list in a restaurant. To choose which dish we would like to eat, our mind must first understand what everything on the menu actually is, what it means, how it tastes, and whether we like it or not.

Imagine eating a chocolate cake or an apple. Imagine biting into it, the taste in your mouth, the texture and its smell. When you imagine swallowing it, how do you feel?

To understand even that simple sentence, your mind flicks through your internal manual, (your mind map) and locates the section labelled "food".

If you have ever eaten a piece of chocolate cake or tasted an apple, then your mind will quickly be able to re-experience its taste, and through the reference structure of your five senses your mind will then replay the experience to you and provide you with an emotional feedback to it. We use our past to understand our present, but also to predict our future.

This mental manual doesn't just provide us with a record of our past memories and experiences, but it also creates a mental expectation of our future too! This is known in NLP as a time line.

Rookie Buster

We use our past to understand our present, but also to predict our future.

An introduction to time lines

Your time line is a mental collection of your experiences, memories, emotions, experienced learning and understandings. This information is held in structured sequential format, dating back from the day you

32   are born, up until this point right now. However, to enable your subconscious mind to continually function with direction and purpose
(without needing constant guidance from your conscious mind), your
mind expands this time line forward as well. Your internal mind map
has a time line that travels from the day you were born, right up until
the day you die.

Your time line can operate from behind you through to in front of
you (hence the saying, "your past is behind you and the future lies
ahead"):

Future
Present
Past

Or it can operate from your left through to your right:

Past   Present   Future

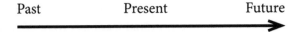

This internal manual has a blueprint, highlighting every element of
your future mental diary for the coming week, months and years. It
contains all your points of interest, a "to-do" list and even the mile-
stones to compare your progress against.

Using your time line

Test your own time line by answering these questions:
- What do you want to achieve at work next week?
- What will you wear, who are you likely to meet and what are you
  going to do at the end of the day?
- Where are you going to be in the New Year?
- What are you going to be doing on your next holiday?
- Where are you going?
- How will you know when you've got there?
- Who's going with you?

On reading those questions, your mind should easily be able to answer at least 5 or 6 of them.

Obviously nothing is set in stone, and we may consciously choose to alter certain details, elements or events within our plans, but the fact still remains, that right now your subconscious mind has a fair estimation of what it is you are going to be doing and where it is you are going to be doing it, for quite some time to come.

Your mind is able to do this because of a magical little world called daydreaming. That's right, daydreaming – the thing we will all have been told off for doing at least once in our lifetime. But when we daydream, we are actually training our minds into creating our future.

Rookie Buster

When we daydream, we are actually training our minds into creating our future.

We constantly use our brilliant imagination to plan out everything, all the tiny elements of what we will be doing, how we will be doing it, who'll be there, how we'll feel and why we think it's a good idea to do it in the first place.

When we sit and plan our working day, we use our imagination to construct, list and remember all the various jobs that we have to do, the order in which we'll have to do them and the reason (the "why") behind doing them. We then refer to our past similar experiences and utilize our past understanding to provide us with the patterned examples of how we go about performing the automatic functions on our "to do" list, mentally cutting and pasting the structure together to fit our needs and amending it if necessary.

34   Every time we daydream, we create a new pathway on our future internal map, and the difference between the daydreams that remain just dreams and the ones that become our reality is all down to our expectations. Our expectations become our reality and we drive our expectations through our beliefs.

Rookie Buster

> Our expectations become our reality and we drive our expectations through our beliefs.

And the daydreams that we believe and expect to happen... often will.

Every time you plan anything in your mind, you are essentially daydreaming. When you daydream, you create a reality and an image on your internal time line, your mental map, detailing where you need to go and what you need to do. Once this image, this plan, is on your map, if you mix in a little element of expectation, then your subconscious gains all the ingredients necessary to automatically steer you into that reality. You've mentally cut and pasted the programs needed, you know what to expect when you're there, and now you don't really have to consciously analyse anything; your subconscious will do the rest.

The downside to this way of working is that anything you expect to happen, and that you daydream, plan and create a map for, will in due course come about! It's important therefore to choose your thoughts carefully; otherwise you may find your dreams are actually becoming your nightmares.

Our internal maps provide our subconscious with the understanding it needs to function automatically. The more we practise daydreaming all the details of our desired reality, the more ingrained that reality becomes on our map and the stronger the chances become that our subconscious will turn it into reality.

Daydreaming your reality

Your conscious mind can only deal with a limited amount of information, so if you spend all your time playing the daydream game of what if, do you choose something positive or something negative?

Whatever you focus all of your attention upon and map out all the tiny details for, will inevitably become your reality.

Go back to the question "What would you do if you knew you couldn't fail?"

Now imagine your outcome, your goal.

- How will you feel when you achieve it?
- How will you know you are there?
- What will you see, hear and feel?
- Who is with you?
- What does it mean for you to be here?
- What impact does it have upon your life?
- What steps do you need to begin taking in order for you to achieve it?

Spend at least five minutes a day daydreaming about this reality. Feel it, hear it, see it and, most importantly, believe it will happen.

Our subconscious mind doesn't like the unknown. Everything our subconscious does is an automatic response and an automatic program. Our subconscious relies upon our internal map to guide it through our daily life and into our future. If your plan is not etched upon your map of expectation, then your subconscious mind will refuse to acknowledge it.

Rookie Buster

Our subconscious mind doesn't like the unknown.

It's all very well wanting to become confident when giving a

36   presentation, or craving the motivation to become self employed, but unless you've ever experienced it or spent a decent amount of time daydreaming it into reality and on to your time line, your subconscious mind will have no reference of it, and no understood learning or program to follow.

Coach's notes

A little make-believing

When we play make-believe as children, we are not just playing but also learning, practising and preparing our mind with the skills we want for the future.

1. Think of something you want to achieve, would like to do or maybe something that you want to be – "I want to be a top sales executive."

2. Imagine what qualities you will need to achieve this, and what resources you need to get – tools (a car), training (an NLP course), emotional resources (confidence, ambition, etc.).

3. Spend a couple of minutes imagining how you will be once you have gained all of your required resources. What will you hear, what will you see and how will you feel? Maybe: "I will be listening to the radio, whilst driving in my new blue sports car to the exclusive golf club I have recently joined. I will be feeling incredibly happy because I've just been paid my large monthly bonus and that means I can now afford to go on this fantastic cruise around the Caribbean."

4. Bring your thoughts to the here and now and imagine what it would be like if you already had all the resources you needed now – confidence, ambition, etc. What difference would it make having these skills now? What impact would it have on your life now?

5. Become aware of your goal and start pretending for ten minutes every day that you have already achieved it (this does not mean spending lots of money you don't have!). Imagine you already have all the resources you need; how are you choosing to use and apply them?
6. Now become aware and take the first steps towards turning your make believe into your reality. Spend ten minutes every day make believing you already have the qualities, the resources or the life you want to lead. Provide your subconscious with the basic understanding, the program and the foundations of learning, so it can begin implementing the steps to create your amazing reality.

Go for it! Your expectations in life will become your reality, and these expectations are created through your thoughts, your dreams, your plans and, more importantly, your imagination. Learn to become aware of what it is you are actually planning for your subconscious mind. Through your awareness you can take control of and also responsibility for your own future. Do you choose a reality based on the foundations of dreams, or of nightmares?

40 Notes

Notes

In this chapter you will learn how the brain processes and interprets surrounding information through the various senses: auditory, kinaesthetic, visual, gustatory and olfactory (or hearing, touch, sight, taste and smell). We will understand the impact our "representational filters" have upon the way we interpret language and how it can affect our communication with one another. We will also introduce "submodalities" and the effect they can have on our ideas and memories, and how manipulating them can alter the influence of our thoughts.

CHAPTER 3

What you see isn't always what other people get!

Representational systems

Any business wanting to operate on an international level must be aware that not only do their potential clients, customers and colleagues speak in a different language, but also their cultures, traditions and methodologies may be significantly different as well.

The body language used within Western culture can often convey a completely opposite meaning within Eastern culture. In Western culture, direct eye contact is a sign of confidence, interest and honesty, while in many Eastern countries it is actually considered to be highly disrespectful, rude and arrogant. Imagine the effect this could have in a business meeting, if you had one side of the room trying their utmost to maintain constant eye contact, whilst the other side was doing everything possible to avoid it!

This potential for miscommunication is not just limited to cultural boundaries or national language barriers, however. In the same way that no two people ever perceive the same reality, no two people will ever use the same language of communication.

The seventeenth-century poet John Donne's phrase "No man is an island" would actually be more appropriate if you changed the "No" to an "Every" and then applied that to how we all think: "Every man is an island". Here we all are, living on our own separate islands, each experiencing our own different weather, different scenery, different cultures, language, beliefs, manners, phone and postal systems, everybody perceiving their own personal version of life. How many messages do you think would get lost due to poor translation issues, bad phone reception or simply because of the infrequent mail deliveries between the islands?

Rookie Buster

In the same way that no two people ever perceive the same reality, no two people will ever use the same language of communication.

Often when things go wrong within business, when deals are lost or conflicts in the workplace occur, it is because of poorly transmitted or translated communication.

We have all had those moments when we have experienced instant rapport with someone. They could be a complete stranger, but from the moment conversation began, for some reason we knew immediately that they were seeing eye to eye with us. We may even have gone as far as to describe them as being on our wavelength. We have also all probably experienced speaking with another person whom we simply couldn't connect with, however hard we tried, leaving us feeling as though this was because they probably "couldn't see where we were coming from".

All of our interaction and communication with the world begins with our thoughts, and our thoughts are represented to us through our senses. We use our senses to collect, understand and utilize all the information that is presented to us both internally and externally.

Rookie Buster

All of our interaction and communication with the world begins with our thoughts, and our thoughts are represented to us through our senses.

Through our individual lives we have each learned to use these senses differently, often choosing to prioritize one sense over the others (known in NLP as your "primary sense"). Bear in mind that we are using our senses to understand information from the world, and to communicate it and our thoughts to one another. Imagine what would happen if one person began communicating to another using just visual language and the other person responded by using just auditory language. They would very quickly find that, although some similar words may be used and recognized, the meaning behind the communication would probably be misrepresented, misunderstood or simply lost in translation from one sensory language to another.

We are all born with five senses, sight, sound, touch, taste and smell (or visual, auditory, kinaesthetic, gustatory and olfactory), which in NLP terms are referred to as our "representational systems".

Representational systems explained

Anyone wanting to learn how to communicate better, whether in business or socially, will benefit tremendously by mastering the communicative language of the representational system. Understanding this system provides a demonstrative insight into how people think and provides us with a valuable tool for rapport, empathy and influence.

46

Rookie Buster

Anyone wanting to learn how to communicate better, whether in business or socially, will benefit tremendously by mastering the communicative language of the representational system.

The five senses

As a general rule we all have five senses through which we can explore and interpret the world in which we live. Within Western culture, however, there is a tendency to rely mainly upon just three of those five senses, the visual, auditory and kinaesthetic (sight, sound and touch). We will concentrate on just those three here, but do be aware that the other two senses are just as important and useful, as it is only through your awareness of them all that you can truly experience the rich tapestry of information available to you in every second and enjoy the full symphony that your senses can create.

Visual – what we see and imagine

Your visual sense handles and decodes all the information (images) you observe with your eyes (see), as well as the pictures and mental images you create within your mind's eye (imagination).

Visual people have a tendency to talk quickly, using a higher pitch of tonality. Their breathing is fairly shallow, and they can also suffer from slight muscle tension around their shoulders, as they tend to hold their body fairly upright.

Auditory – what we hear and listen to, both externally (noise, sounds) and internally (our internal dialogue)

Your auditory sense focuses upon the sounds within your surrounding environment and listens to

information externally through your ears and internally through your 47
internal dialogue. (Your internal dialogue is the voice inside your head
that is currently reading this sentence to you.)

Auditory people tend to use an expressive voice and tone, their
speech is evenly paced and their head sits fairly balanced upon their
shoulders. You know when auditory people are listening to you or
themselves, as they often tilt their head to one side while listening.

Kinaesthetic – feelings, touch

Your kinaesthetic sense understands how you feel in response to your
environment, and is operated through your sense of touch, your internal feelings and your emotions.

Kinaesthetic people will continuously check in with their emotions
to guide their words, and this often results in them speaking quite
slowly, while occasionally stopping for long pauses. Their head is often
down and their breathing is relaxed and generally deep.

Gustatory – recognizes all the various tastes

Olfactory – acknowledges all the different smells

The primary sense

As we experience the external world, we will use all our five senses to
varying degrees, although over time we often begin to favour one sense
(our primary sense, or primary system) over the other two. We choose
our primary system for many reasons. Often it is a reflection of our
interests or career choices: a musician may be auditory, a footballer
may be kinaesthetic, or a fashion designer may be visual. The development of our primary system often takes place around our teenage
years, but it can also be influenced by our daily lives.

Take the example of a journalist who has progressed her career to
becoming an editor. She may originally have been very visual in her
sensory preference, and brilliant when it came to her use of words, cap-
turing and retelling the details of her story in print. Years

48 of proofreading may now have left her with a primary system that is auditory, probably because her job has required her to learn to listen to how words flow, focusing her attention more upon the rhythm and structure of language, rather than its visual content. The end result of this development is a switch from a visual preference to an auditory one.

Why is it important to hone our primary sense to match our environment?

If we focus more of our attention into one primary sense, it can often serve us better when operating a specific function. A well-trained primary sense can pick out more of the relevant details within a piece of information, which can be very important if your particular interest or job requires you to notice minute differences or perceive finer distinctions between things. For example, a surgeon may need to be very kinaesthetic, and a musician acutely auditory.

So in the case of our journalist, by honing her auditory skills she has become more proficient in hearing the subtle differences of poorly used sentence structures, a change in grammatical rhythm or the sound resonating within wrongly chosen words. The point being, a trained editor is far more likely to spot subtle differences within a text than a kinaesthetically trained physiotherapist is.

Just because we operate a primary sense doesn't mean we are limited to using only that sense. If we train our mind to recognize the qualities and uses of the different senses, we can soon learn how to alternate between them. This knowledge gives us the ability to select the sense that will prove more suitable for reflecting and representing our environment and the tasks we want to perform, and enabling us to communicate with others effectively.

Rapport through representational systems

Because we often use language to communicate our thoughts, it is the first thing you should pay attention to. When attempting to recognize someone's primary sense, all the information you need can be found within the words that they are using.

Rookie Buster

When attempting to recognize someone's primary sense, all the information you need can be found within the words that they are using.

Visual (understanding information through images and pictures)
Uses these words and phrases:

See, look, picture, focus, notice, insight.

"I can see what you mean," "We see eye to eye," "Show me what you mean," "Picture this..."

Auditory (understanding information through sounds that we hear)
Uses these words and phrases:

Say, rhythm, tone, discuss, hear, speechless, listen.

"I can hear what you are saying," "Music to my ears," "Loud and clear," "On the same wavelength."

Kinaesthetic (understanding information through our feeling and touch)
Uses these words and phrases:

Touch, solid, sensitive, cold, harsh, tangible.

"I have a gut feeling about that," "Can't put my finger on it," "Thick skinned."

In business, especially in sales, understanding your customer's language of thought is of paramount importance if you want to ensure your meaning reaches them with maximum impact and influence. Learning to recognize someone's primary representational system will provide key clues into how we can begin creating rapport and gaining empathy from our audience.

We immediately gain rapport with people who make us feel as though they think in the same way as us, that they empathize with what we are saying and that they truly understand us.

50

Rookie Buster

We immediately gain rapport with people who make us feel as though they think in the same way as us.

If we present our ideas and intentions in the language style that mirrors our intended audience's thinking preferences, they are more likely to recreate our meaning in a way that is tangible to them and in a way that maintains the intent behind our communication.

Presentations

If you are communicating with more than one individual, perhaps presenting to an audience, then it is a good idea to practise mixing your language sensory styles to incorporate the entire primary thinking systems.

Good communication is often not *what* you say but *how* you say it.

Rookie Buster

Good communication is often not *what* you say but *how* you say it.

As well as being able to hear the way people think by listening to their specific language styles, we can also gain visible clues into another person's thought process.

The human mind and body are intrinsically linked and operate as one holistic system, which means whatever is happening in one part is often reflected within the other. Every thought you think affects your body, and your body affects the way that you think. I can see what you

are thinking, as it's written all over your face! So our eyes can truly be   51
the windows to our souls, or at least into our thought processes.

Neurological studies have shown that as we think our many complex
and different thoughts (visual, auditory, kinaesthetic), our eyes actually reflect these thoughts, moving in specific directions that corre-
spond to the stimulation going on within the different parts of our
brain.

In NLP terms, these movements are known as "eye accessing cues".

Eye accessing cues are another useful way of gleaning insight into
another person's thought processes and, like sensory language, they
will with enough practice help you understand the quickest approach
to adopt in your communication.

Eye accessing cues

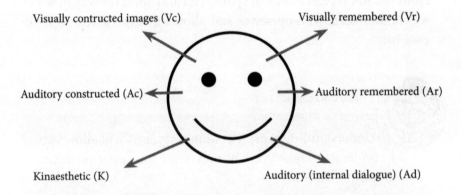

A good salesman will recognize the importance of his communication
when it comes to influencing a customer's buying strategy. Not only
must he build rapport and elicit their wants and buying motivation,
but he must also then present the product in a way that the customer
can emotionally and positively respond to. By recognizing the customer's primary sense, whether it is auditory, visual or kinaesthetic,
the flexible salesman can adapt his sales pitch and represent his product
in a way that reflects the customer's thought processes and point of
influence.

Eye accessing cues are something you should practise with a partner
before implementing, as the cues happen very quickly, and staring at

52   your clients may not quite create the impression you were aiming for.

Recognizing people's representational systems is a key factor in effective communication; but it is also important for us to recognize their influence upon our own performance.

Submodalities

Remember, every thought we have is represented to us via our senses, and it is because of these thoughts that we recreate our memories, develop our ambitions and provide the foundations for our directional behaviour.

Understanding representational systems will allow you to understand how you can maximize the impact of your communication. However, our representational system can also affect the way in which we communicate with ourselves and allow our experiences to influence us.

Rookie Buster

Understanding representational systems will allow you to understand how you can maximize the impact of your communication.

Our representational system provides our mind with a methodology for understanding and replaying all the information around us. This information is then further broken down, coded and stored in our minds through our sensory modalities, called "submodalities".

It is these submodalities that give our memories, images and thoughts deeper meaning, and if we really want to start creating change in ourselves and others, it is important for us to recognize the impact that submodalities can have.

Every thought is comprised of a submodality structure, and by learning to manipulate these submodalities we can influence our response to experiences, memories, dreams, nightmares, habits and ambitions.

If you were to watch a horror movie about a girl walking downstairs in broad daylight and discovering a dead body at the bottom, it might be horrible, but it would be over very quickly, it would be unlikely to have a long lasting impact upon you, and it would definitely struggle in the cinemas. However, if the scene was filmed in near darkness, with eerie music, the sounds of wind rustling in the trees and creaking floorboards, and close-ups of the heroine looking apprehensive and then terrified, the film would take on a whole different feel, would stir up our emotion and create a completely different impact upon us.

Submodalities are the equivalent of our mind having its own camera crew and production team. They provide our brain with its own personal cinematic experience of light, sound and emotive effects.

Rookie Buster

Submodalities are the equivalent of our mind having its own camera crew and production team.

If you want to make a memory stronger or sell an idea with more impact, it is important to recognize that it is our submodalities that truly cause us to emotively respond to language. Submodalities make an image real, alive and tangible, and give it the influence to alter our reactions. And by altering the submodalities of a thought, you will also alter its impact.

You can also make bad thoughts less scary. For example, imagine watching the same horror movie, but with a Disney theme tune instead

54 of eerie music, bright colours instead of dark shadows, and a dog's squeaky toy instead of creaking floorboards. Doesn't have quite the same effect now, does it?

Or equally you can make happy memories stronger and more appealing.

Our memories hold an influence over our behaviour, not because of the actual event, but because of the way we choose to replay the experience.

Exercise: Altering the submodalities

In your imagination, think now of any memory that makes you happy.
- When you think of this memory, do you see pictures (visual)?
- How bright is the picture?
- Is it close to you or far away?
- Is it moving or still?
- Are you associated to the picture (inside it)?
- Or disassociated (outside and looking in)?
- Do you have a feeling or a sensation (kinaesthetic)?
- Where are the feeling located?
- Is it strong or soft?
- Moving or still?
- Are there any sounds that you are aware of (auditory)?
- Where are they located?
- Are they loud or soft?
- Is there any music; are there any voices?
- Can you any hear words being said and how do they sound?

Once you have established all the submodalities of your memory, choose one element to alter.
- If you are seeing a picture, what happens if you make it brighter?
- What happens if you make the picture bigger and closer?
- If you are disassociated (outside and looking in, i.e. as a 3rd person) what do you notice happens when you step in and associate with the picture (i.e. becoming the 1st person)?

Coach's notes

What language are we all speaking?

Remember, everyone may appear to be using the same words, but the language and the interpretation of this language isn't always the same.

Recognizing someone's representational system will allow your communication to become much more effective.

1. Once a day, actively choose to try and uncover which representational system someone else is using. Make a note of how they portray their system. What words do they use to describe their experiences, thoughts, feelings? Where do their eyes move to when they are thinking and speaking?

2. Once you have become aware of their specific representational system, try and alter your own representational system to mirror theirs. What do you notice happens? How does the individual now respond to you?

3. Now deliberately alter your representational system to *mismatch* against theirs. What do you notice happens? How does the individual now respond to you?

4. Spend five minutes actively training your senses every day. Try observing the world using a different representational system, choosing to alternate once in a while from the one you normally use. How different does the world appear and how differently do people respond to you?

Go for it! Pay attention and learn to understand your own mind's submodalities: become the movie producer of your own thoughts, and choose what impact you want the film of your life to have upon you. Is it going to be a romantic comedy to inspire and amuse, a Disney film with a happy ending, or perhaps a horror movie that instils paralysing fears and phobias in you? Learning to manipulate your submodalities is a great way of tackling phobias, enhancing happy memories or removing the negative impact of your bad experiences.

Notes

Whether you are in recruitment, telesales or management, a sole trader or a company CEO, the ability to create and maintain good rapport with those around you is paramount to your success. Unfortunately, rapport is not something you can turn on and off at will; you either have it or you don't, and without it, the world of business is not the business to be in. In this chapter we are going to learn about rapport, how to recognize it, and its importance in business, and also learn the strategies behind creating it.

CHAPTER 4

People buy people

Rapport

No business can operate without communication, and effective communication can only take place once a strong sense of rapport has been established. To buy into someone else's ideas, opinion or influence, we must first buy into them, and this involves creating a strong element of trust and perceived mutual understanding and respect.

If you think about the people whom you've allowed to influence you and your decisions, what quality is it they possess that attracts you towards them, and what makes you buy into their concept again and again?

The friends we choose, as well as bosses, colleagues, clients, teachers, coaches, retailers and sales people, all of these individuals have the ability to influence your opinions, your thoughts and your subsequent decisions, and recognizing this will allow you to begin purposefully influencing them in turn.

However, before anyone is able to influence anything, we must first establish a baseline of trust. Trust is paramount if any relationship is to exist, and can only be created through established rapport. Without rapport we have nothing but meaningless words and actions.

So what is rapport and how do you know when you have it and when you don't?

Rookie Buster

Trust is paramount if any relationship is to exist, and can only be created through established rapport.

Where does rapport come from?

Rapport is the seamless communication between individuals, and it is created as soon as a mutual connection and understanding is made and conversation becomes allowed to just flow.

Words do not have to exist for rapport to exist. According to the research conducted by Professor Mehrabian of the University of California at Los Angeles (UCLA), 55 per cent of all our communication is body language, 38 per cent is tonality, and only 7 per cent actually consists of the words that we say. Even those words are further subjected to representational system translation (sensory language) and perceptions (beliefs and values).

Every single action, facial expression, sigh, posture, tone, rhythm and hand gesture creates an impression and communicates an idea. Your mind and body are one and neither can exist without influencing the other.

This means that whatever thoughts we are thinking internally in our minds will always be reflected upon our external physiology. You cannot not communicate!

Have you ever experienced a time when you were tempted to buy

something, but then found yourself being put off because the salesperson was incredibly obnoxious or simply appeared uninterested in selling to you? What quality was it about them that made you change your mind?

Remember, as individuals we respond to the world through our perceptions and our judgements, and any decisions or actions we take are driven by our values and beliefs.

Everyone, no matter who they are or how important others perceive them to be, likes to feel acknowledged and valued. Our opinions count, our feelings matter, and we believe that we are worthwhile enough to expect respect from others, whether it be in the work place, at a conference or in the high street.

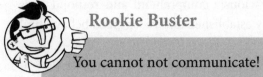

Rookie Buster

You cannot not communicate!

If we believe someone is uninterested in our thoughts, our wants or our needs, we reject them. There is no respect and no understanding, and fundamentally no rapport, which means no matter what the other person has to offer, the chances are we are very unlikely to choose to hear them out or respond to anything they have to say.

In fact, have you ever noticed that the more you dislike a person, the more likely you are to do the very opposite of what it is they have asked of you?

No relationship can exist without rapport. If you want to influence your boss into offering you that promotion, the interviewers into giving you that job, or your client into buying your product over your competitors, then you must first establish a relationship of trust, understanding and rapport.

Rapport is not something you can just switch on and off at will, it is something you have to create, and sometimes that may mean becom-

61

62   ing flexible in your own behaviour and angles of perception.

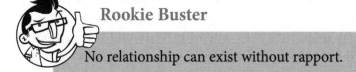

Rookie Buster

No relationship can exist without rapport.

Rapport exists on a subconscious level, and it is a major part of the 93 per cent of our non-verbal communication. Rapport also works on various levels within the human psyche. From our brain's point of view, everything we subconsciously comprehend and respond to is strongly linked to our already established and recognized behavioural patterns.

This means, if your subconscious mind notices another person demonstrating a similar gesture, facial expression, tone of voice or even a shared opinion, your subconscious mind will automatically acknowledge a similarity between the two of you and therefore create a link. This perceived similarity becomes enough for you then to begin feeling as though you understand what the other person is thinking, leading you then to believe you now share some common ground of thought. This creates a feeling of unity, perceived mutual understanding and eventually, should more similarities continue to be noticed, a deep level of trust and rapport is established.

At another level, human beings like to feel part of a group and accepted. It makes us feel safe and allows us to feel confident within our thoughts and actions. If our subconscious notices our subconscious communication being reciprocated, mirrored and responded to, then this is seen subconsciously as a mark of acceptance and again of unity.

"Towards" and "away from"

One thing that is phenomenally important to remember, especially if what you are aiming for requires you to be liked by the other person (and this is very important in sales, presentations and interviews), is the basic "towards" and "away from" strategies and how to apply them to basic attraction.

We are all drawn towards things that make us feel good and away from things that make us feel bad. There is a reason why you don't put your hand over a flame, jump out of a ten-storey building without the use of a bungee cord, or stick your fingers into the company paper shredder, and this is because we are all incredibly hard wired to avoid pain or anything we believe will be unpleasant to us – including people.

Rookie Buster

> We are all drawn towards things that make us feel good and away from things that make us feel bad.

If you think about the people you choose to spend time with, whose company you enjoy, what is it about these people that makes you want to keep seeing them again and again?

Some reasons you may come up with are: they make you laugh or smile; you feel comfortable in their company; you respect that person's opinion and feel as though you learn from them; you feel brighter, smarter with them, etc. Whatever the specific reason, there will be some quality about that person that leaves you feeling good on one level or another, a perceived gain.

Now, think of another person, someone whom you would do everything possible to avoid. This includes hiding yourself away in the works storeroom cupboard or crossing the street just to avoid spending time with them. This type of person is the kind of individual who makes your heart sink, your blood boil, or maybe leaves you feeling fearful, inadequate or just simply depressed. When you think of this person, what quality do they possess that makes you want to avoid them at all costs?

The chances are that these people leave you feeling insecure, unsettled, angry, upset, frightened, negative, pessimistic, and so on. These people probably demonstrate a specific quality that leaves you feeling negative on one level or another, and you perceive a sense of loss when you're with them.

Imagine a client has two salespeople knocking on his door, both selling exactly the same product at the same price. How does the client choose which one to buy from?

Salesperson A is very professionally presented and articulate, but can only ever discuss business and make small talk about the weather.

Salesperson B's tie isn't fastened properly and his shirt is none too clean, but he has an easy sense of humour, remembers that the client likes to watch football and spent most of his sales pitch time discussing last night's football game, only briefly mentioning the product once as he leaves.

Who do you think the client chooses to buy from?

The client chooses salesperson B in this scenario, as the client enjoyed his company more. Because the nature of the business required regular contact with his supplier (the salesperson), the client decided to choose someone whose company he would enjoy on a regular basis.

This scenario could have gone the other way if the client had valued appearance over company, which is why it is important to elicit an individual's values and beliefs before attempting to influence their opinion.

Rookie Buster

It is important to elicit an individual's values and beliefs before attempting to influence their opinion.

People who are very successful in creating strong rapport with other people are usually individuals who have understood the attraction element behind rapport. Attraction is not about who you actually are, but about how the other person perceives you to be and how you make them feel within themselves. If someone feels good in your company, they will come back to you again and again, selecting you over others, and this leaves you in a very powerful position of influence.

How can you recognize rapport?

It is obvious when two people are in rapport, as their body language can be observed demonstrating a mutual dance of gestures, rhythm, postures and expressions.

Have you ever noticed two people locked away in deep conversation with one another? The way the eye contact is held, how one person's body mirrors the other, the rise and fall of their tonality, and also the way in which everyone else in the room seems to be leaving them to it, no one daring to intrude upon their deep discussion.

Creating rapport

To create rapport you must start from genuine interest and respect, and you must feel confident in your own personal values and beliefs, outcomes and identity, but also flexible in your perceptions to understand another's point of view.

66 A matching and mirroring exercise

Matching yourself into another's style of communication is one of the quickest ways to establish rapport, and it resonates well with the subconscious need for recognizing and linking similar patterns. However, you must remember you want to *match* the other person's behaviour – not mimic them.

Rookie Buster

You must remember you want to *match* the other person's behaviour – not mimic them.

Things that you would aim to match:
- Physiology – Gestures, body posture, movement, positions and expressions.
- Breathing – The pace.
- Tonality and pace – The musical sound of the voice when talking, loud, soft, high, deep.
- Language – Key words or representational systems.
- Values, beliefs or opinions – The ideals the individual holds important.
- Experiences – Are there any shared experiences or passions?

To build rapport
Ask a partner to practise this with you.
1. Notice the breathing first, the rise and fall of their chest. (Get your partner to move their hand up and down as they breathe to provide you with a visual cue.)
2. Begin pacing your breathing to theirs, inhaling and exhaling when they do.
3. Ask your partner to talk about something they are passionate about.

- Notice the language they use – key phrases, representational systems.
- Notice they way in which they stand – for example, are their arms folded?
- Notice if they make a lot of eye contact – do they look away a lot or hold your gaze?
- Notice what are they talking about – is there something there you can relate to?
- Listen to the sound of the voice – slow, loud, fast.

4. Once you have elicited enough of their key qualities, choose three to use and reflect back to them.
5. Begin your communication with them, matching your chosen three gestures and mirroring their breathing, and do this until you feel comfortable.

To create strong rapport, you must be sincere in your intentions and take an active and genuine interest in the other person's point of view. Respect and acknowledge their perceptions, even though they may be completely different from your own. To influence someone, you must go to his or her side of the fence first.

Rookie Buster

To influence someone, you must go to his or her side of the fence first.

Pacing and leading

Once we've established basic rapport, we are then in a position to begin influencing the other person with our ideas and perception or towards implementing change.

Learning the ability of pacing and leading is a key skill in sales and business meetings, one-to-one interviewing, deal closure or any

68 situation that requires you to introduce a new subject matter or a new way of thinking (potentially yours).

Pacing

When you pace another person, you are looking for confirmation or feedback that the other person is in mutual rapport with you. Pacing is an ongoing process and involves constantly matching and checking in with another person's level of rapport in response to you. It involves careful matching and mirroring, listening, checking for feedback that you are truly in rapport with the other person and operating within their reality, and that there is a mutual exact understanding of the intent that is being communicated back and forth.

If in doubt, pace, pace and pace again!

To check if you are in rapport and that you have achieved a strong level of trust within the individual, you should first test it before attempting to lead them in another direction of thinking.

Exercise: Testing to lead

1. After you have spent time mirroring your individual and you feel that you have a strong connection and a good rapport established, change one of your gestures from mirroring into something new. So, if you have been using your arms to talk, now cross them. It is important to keep everything else in rapport, so if you have been maintaining eye contact, continue to do so, and if you have been reflecting gestures or mutual opinions, continue to do so. You do not want to break rapport; you are simply testing the structure.
2. Now hold this new position for a while and notice if your partner also changes their posture to mirror into yours. Do they now fold their arms too?
3. Once you have a positive result, test it further by changing one more element, and observe the response. If it is positive, your partner is now ready to be led into your way of thinking.

Leading

When you feel you have established strong rapport, you have checked it and paced it again and again, you are now ready to change the direction of the conversation, alter the focus of communication and begin heading in the direction that reflects your desired outcome.

A clever way of introducing new concepts or ideas is by linking them to already established ideas and connecting them to the current conversation.

For example, a recruitment firm that one of us worked with suddenly found themselves operating within a market that was experiencing a recession. This meant that there were now far more candidates (due to redundancies) than there were jobs to fill, and also more recruitment consultants working on these limited jobs, causing the working culture to become much more aggressive.

The MD of the company was aware that the working environment had changed, and to ensure his company survived, he needed to retrain his staff, so they knew how to recruit in a recession.

This is what the MD did.

MD's desired outcome – introduce new training

MD: So, how well do you think we are doing at the moment?

STAFF 1: OK, but not as well as we were last month; interview numbers are down.

STAFF 2: It's not for lack of trying, though. We have spent all day hammering the phones, but no one seems interested.

MD: I recognize you are all working hard, and yes, you're right, interview numbers are down from last month. Why do you think that is?

STAFF 1: I imagine it's a sign of what's to come; there are less jobs about and no one wants to pay our fees any more.

70   MD: Is there anything we could do to change that?

STAFF 2: I don't know, I've been trying everything I know and nothing seems to be working.

MD: I agree you've never worked in a recession before. Do you think the reason why what we're doing isn't working is because the market has changed?

STAFF 2: I'm sure that's the reason.

MD: In that case do you think we should adapt our working methodology to reflect the new market?

STAFF 1: The only way any company can evolve is by having the ability to adapt.

MD: I agree. How about we do some group retraining?

When we want to influence someone's focus of communication into a new direction, it is easier if we link into their current train of thought and then use this understanding to guide them into a new direction.

Remember: rapport first; then pace, pace and pace again; then lead – and then add a little more pacing, just for good measure.

Rookie Buster

Remember: rapport first; then pace, pace and pace again; then lead – and then add a little more pacing, just for good measure.

Coach's notes

There are many different ways of building rapport. Practise these:
1. Make a list of all the different ways you could choose to establish rapport with someone in the following situations:
   - In a one-to-one meeting.
   - Over the phone.
   - Over the internet.
   - At a party.
   - Whilst delivering a presentation.
2. Once you have created your list, actively practise using them as often as possible.

Which methods do you find are the most effective for you?

Go for it! A smile can say a thousand words and it doesn't cost anything. A smile is very similar to a yawn – it is very influential and very hard not to reciprocate. It is also one of the most popular anchors for creating happy states in others, because when you smile you release endorphins (the happy hormone) into the blood stream. Smiling can instil confidence, create relaxation and defuse many a situation, and better still, it doesn't cost you anything.

Notes

Beliefs can have wonderfully creative or a terribly destructive effect upon our lives. They are the stuff of dreams and success, of nightmares and wars. In this chapter we will truly tap into the motivational elements of NLP and gain insight into our own belief structure, its limitations and its infinite potential. You will learn how your value system operates, and why we make the decisions we do. Uncover what is truly important to you and how to access it more effectively and quickly. This chapter will explain how and why our beliefs play a major part in our success and our failures, and will give you the exercises necessary to begin changing this.

CHAPTER 5

Is it important and do you believe it?

Beliefs

The ability to make appropriate judgement calls and effective decisions is a quality any businessperson must have if they want to lead their company towards success and far away from failure. And the difference between a successful billionaire and an average entrepreneur is often a profound quality called belief.

What would you attempt if you believed you could never fail?

There are certain behavioural qualities that we can all recognize would benefit particular elements of our working, personal and social lives. These can be things such as confidence, creativity, presentation skills, social skills, linguistics, pro-activity, courage, dynamic thinking, management skills, organization... The list can go on and on.

One of the main qualities that set an excellent salesman apart from an average one is something called confidence – confidence in their product, confidence in their knowledge of and ability to sell that product, and, more importantly, confidence within themselves.

Rookie Buster

One of the main qualities that set an excellent salesman apart from an average one is something called confidence.

Where does this confidence come from? What quality creates that fearless instinct?

The answer is self-belief.

Belief systems

Our belief system is one of the most powerful influences on our perception and behaviour. Every day, deals are won and lost off the back of beliefs. Wars are started, promotions achieved, major businesses launched and careers held back, all because of the system we operate under, called our belief structure.

Remember, our conscious mind can only comprehend a limited amount of information at any one time (five, seven or nine pieces of it), and it is through this limited perception that we focus and choose what information to base our reality upon. Our perception, our choices, judgements, decisions and all subsequent behaviours are guided by our beliefs and our values. Whatever you believe to be true, is.

Our beliefs are the things in life that we know to be true, although they are not actually based upon any real, factual evidence. Most beliefs are usually created during our childhood, but they can also be conclusions created from our past experiences, or the influence of shared opinions from other respected individuals (people whom we consider to know better or know more than we do, such as teachers, parents, figures of authority, friends, and so on).

Our expectations in life often influence our beliefs.

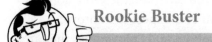

Rookie Buster

Our expectations in life often influence our beliefs.

Endorsement of beliefs

If the very first time you applied for a promotion you were for whatever reason unsuccessful, although you would be disappointed, you might choose to put it down to just bad luck.

If you applied a second time for promotion and again didn't get it, you would probably wonder why, and quite possibly become a little wary of applying a third time.

If you applied a third time there is a strong chance that you would now be feeling sceptical about being offered even an interview, let alone the job itself. If your hunch turned out to be right, then you would probably be left believing that you will never actually be promoted within this company and that it is therefore time either to give up all hope of promotion or at least to begin looking for a job elsewhere.

This is the process known as "endorsement". Because most of our beliefs are installed when we are young, it can only take one strong endorsement for the belief to resonate and become true.

If at school your teacher (a figure in authority) looked over your homework and said, "You are rubbish at maths," and if you looked at your work at that moment, compared it to someone else's and found some confirmation that your teacher was indeed right (as far as you could perceive), your subconscious would then accept the teacher's statement as fact and create a forever restrictive belief that you are indeed rubbish at maths. Having started to believe it, you stop trying

78   (because no one enjoys failing) and then focus your limited attention on things you feel you are better at. And because you stop attempting to improve your maths skills by practising, those skills never improve, meaning that you have created a self-fulfilling prophecy. It's not that you *can't* do it, it's just that you *believe* you can't, and therefore don't try – and unless you practise, how can you ever expect to improve?

Because beliefs influence our perceptions and motivations, they are often fairly difficult to change. And most beliefs tend to become self-fulfilling prophecies.

Rookie Buster

Most beliefs tend to become self-fulfilling prophecies.

Since our perceptual filters select the information we choose to take on board, the information our mind chooses to focus upon will consequently only ever be the information that reflects and resonates with our current belief system. This means that the only information your subconscious allows you to become aware of is the evidence to back up the belief, therefore making it near impossible to disprove.

Positive beliefs

But our beliefs are not only negative – they can be positive too. If you believe you *can* do something, then the chances are you will keep trying until you find a way to succeed. This is often the belief system driving successful entrepreneurs. Because they truly believe in their ideas, their entrepreneurial skills and their drive, and honestly believe that they are destined to be successful, they will hone their perceptual filters to allow through only information that reflects this belief. If they make a 79 mistake, they see it as a simple learning curve and not as a failure – in other words, as an example of a way not to do something rather than evidence that they should stop trying and give up.

Your mind has the ability to learn anything. The problem is that we have a tendency to compare ourselves to others and seek external feedback to gauge our progress. Because all our minds our different, they ways in which we take on information and the speeds at which we learn are also different. All of us can learn some things faster than others. This doesn't mean that we can't eventually learn to do everything, only that with some things it may take more time and a little more practice.

Rookie Buster

Your mind has the ability to learn anything.

This doesn't matter when we are younger, as we are not externally aware enough to feel embarrassed about our mistakes, but as we grow older and our need to be accepted and to fit in increases, it starts to matter more. When we find ourselves working at a slower pace than someone else or not understanding something in the way we expect to, or if our attempt is met with ridicule or negative feedback, we very quickly respond with an "away from" strategy and cease attempting to learn the new behaviour, installing instead the new belief that we cannot do it.

Yet there is no such thing as failure – only feedback. We can all learn to walk, talk, eat, read and write, if we are just given the patience and time to learn.

Rookie Buster

There is no such thing as failure – only feedback.

Beliefs direct the focus of our behaviour; they motivate us, guide us and can provide us with a sense of security, belonging and acceptance.

Exercise: Manipulating your beliefs

First think of a belief you know to be true; for example, "I am a great salesman." (If you are struggling to find a belief, use something else you believe or know to be true, such as "The world is round," "There are seven days in the week," and so on.)

Do you get a picture, have a feeling, or hear a sound? What are the submodalities of this belief, the specific qualities creating this sensory experience?

Next think of a belief that is holding you back and that you would like to change; for example, "I am not a confident speaker."

Now superimpose the qualities of the belief that you know to be true on to those of the belief that you would like to change.

Imagine you want to become self employed – what's stopping you?

We cluster our beliefs together to form our belief systems. These systems are then used to support and back up our values. The belief we have in our expectations will always become our reality.

Rookie Buster

The belief we have in our expectations will always become our reality.

Values 81

Our values are the driving forces behind all of our actions and they provide the "why" (the intent) to our behaviour. Every single one of our actions, habits, structures or behavioural patterns began with a value – a reason why to do it and a positive intent. Our values are the driving influences that can motivate or demotivate our behaviour.

We judge all of actions against our values and use them to arrive at conclusions about whether a performed deed was good or bad.

As well as often providing the reason "why" behind our behaviour and our motivations, our values provide focus to our goals and ambitions. Our values give us our reason for being and our sense of purpose in life. Without them we would probably never go out to work, interact with others or even bother to get out of bed in the morning.

How our values start

Most of our values are created throughout our childhood and into our early twenties. We begin originally imprinting our values as a result of our surrounding environment and unconscious learned behaviour. As we develop, we then progress to modelling and learning both consciously and unconsciously as we begin to copy the behaviour and values of our peers, friends, family and adults.

It is during this time that we install some of our fundamental and most deep-rooted values.

Towards our later years, our values become influenced through our experiences with our social environments and our subsequent conclusion. During this time, we learn the importance of relationships, as well as the consequences and influence of our actions upon ourselves and others.

82 The hierarchy of values

We have many different values, all of them varying in their degree of importance and influence. Our values tend to be listed within our subconscious in a hierarchy of importance, which helps to facilitate our decisions when choosing one action over another.

For example – do you decide to get out of the warm, cosy bed and go to work this morning?

- The bed's perceived value: instant gratification of a warm duvet, which makes you feel comfortable and safe.
- Work's value: no instant gratification, but eventually provides the money that buys security and provides freedom. Without it, there would be no nice warm bed to lie in.
- Resulting subconscious decision: to get out of bed and go to work.

Each of our values has its place in a hierarchy of importance.

Rookie Buster

Each of our values has its place in a hierarchy of importance.

Exercise: Uncovering your values

Think of an area in your life that you want to improve. Maybe you're self employed and you want a better work–life balance.

Answer these questions:

- What is important to you in your work?
- What do you gain?
- And what other factors do you think are important to you in this area?

List your answers and then put them into order of importance to you, placing your most important value at the top – for example: 83

1. Acknowledgement.
2. Money.
3. Success.
4. Freedom.
5. Happiness.

Look at your list of values. Are they in the right order or do you need to move the order around? Do your values reflect your ambitions? If you want to spend more time at home, should you maybe swap over "freedom" and "acknowledgement"?

Look at your top three values and consider whether or not they are in conflict with your current behaviour and desires.

You desire spending more time with the family – that means freedom. But because you value acknowledgement and money over this freedom, when you make your subconscious "either or" decision, you will end up choosing something that reflects your current higher value of money, rather than your desired value of freedom. You subconsciously make your decision based upon your current hierarchy of values.

Rookie Buster

You subconsciously make your decision based upon your current hierarchy of values.

This could result in you choosing to spend more time at work than at home, but leave you feeling guilty or resentful because your desires are in conflict with your current values.

If you find you are currently choosing something that is incongruent to your goals, then move your values around.

84 ## Exercise: Changing your values

By choosing to alter your hierarchy of values or adding more suitable ones to your list, you can enhance the values that lead you towards your goals and influence the ones that are holding you back.

You can also change the hierarchy of your values by altering the submodalities (characteristics, images and thoughts) of the values within your mind.

Let's look at the same values as before:

1. Acknowledgement.
2. Money.
3. Success.
4. Freedom.
5. Happiness.

When you think of the value "Freedom", notice the picture or the feelings or sounds in terms of size, colour, position, movement, focus, location, volume, etc.

Now notice the images you create when you think of the value "Money". Next, change the qualities of the images you have for "Freedom", so that they become the same as the ones you have for "Money". This will cause "Freedom" to move to the same level as "Money".

1. Acknowledgement.
2. Money. Freedom.
3. Success.
4. Happiness.

Then change the qualities that you had for "Money" and make them the same as the ones that you previously had for "Freedom". This will cause "Money" to move down to where "Freedom" used to be on your hierarchy structure.

1. Acknowledgement
2. Freedom
3. Success
4. Money
5. Happiness

By altering the order of your values, you will notice that you can 85 influence your subconscious decision-making strategies and change from choosing "work" over "home life", to "home life" over "work".

Our values can be categorized as either an "end" or a "means to" (as in "a means to an end"). "End" values are our subconscious's goals. The "end" value is the aim for all of our behaviour and is the main driving factor behind our ambitions and the subsequent motivation for achieving these ambitions. "Means to" values are the secondary values that lead us towards attaining our "end" value.

"Means to" value	*"End" value*
Better job.	Happiness.
I want to become self employed.	Freedom.
I want to work in a busier working environment.	Love.
I want to be part of a larger firm.	Security.

Coach's notes

Changing beliefs from negative to positive

1. Make a list of all the things in life you would want to do, if you knew you couldn't fail. For example:
   - I want to change my career.
   - I want to be a successful journalist and travel the world.

2. Next to that list, write down everything you believe is preventing you from achieving what you want: I want to change my career, but:
   - I'm not able to do anything else.
   - I'm too old to go back to studying.
   - I need the security of my income.

3. Now, looking at your answers, spend a bit of time working through each one, changing the negative elements so that they become positive.
   - I'm not able to do anything else *changes to* I have the opportunity finally to learn about something I have always been interested in.
   - I'm too old to go back to studying *changes to* I have the maturity to get the most out of my training.
   - I need the security of my income *changes to* I have the opportunity to earn a lot more money.

4. Now re-read your wish list, reading out the new beliefs. Spend some time imagining what would happen if you followed these new beliefs. How do you feel, and what positive differences would it make to your life?

By choosing to change your beliefs, you will change your reality and inevitably obtain your dreams.

Go for it! Learning to understand how your beliefs and values influence your thinking provides you with the insight and knowledge necessary for you to begin taking charge of your actions and deeds.

We respond to the world through our perceptions, and these perceptions are influenced by our beliefs. Once we recognize our beliefs and the intent driving our values, we can choose to change them and take control of our own perceptions and subsequently influence our reality. What would you do in life if you knew you couldn't fail – and what's stopping you? Change the belief, change your reality and obtain your dreams.

Notes

Notes

In this chapter we'll explain how we sort, chunk, relate and respond to our experiences. Every thought and action of ours has an intent driving it and a strategic program operating it. By understanding our strategic (or Meta) programs we can gain insight into our own driving habits as well as those of others. This will teach us how to evaluate our decisions more effectively, communicate more efficiently with others and train our flexibility when it comes to understanding and interacting with other people's individual strategic processes.

CHAPTER 6

Meta programs

Meta programs

Our beliefs and values steer our focus and select the information our subconscious mind chooses to become aware of. Our Meta programs are the systems and patterns we apply when we process, code and react to our gathered information.

Noticing the Meta programs of others is the best way of accessing necessary information that can help us to begin building rapport. This valuable information can be used to guide, motivate, instruct and communicate with ourselves and others on many different and more effective levels. It is also a very valuable tool to use in business, as the Meta programs people operate can have a dramatic impact on their job suitability and satisfaction.

Entrepreneurs, sales people and stockbrokers can often be described as having specific characteristics of language, gestures and beliefs that are common to their professions – characteristics such as being out-going, confident, etc.

People who operate with similar Meta programs will find that they very quickly create rapport when communicating with one another.

92   By matching, mirroring and reflecting someone else's Meta programs we will become able to communicate on an unconscious and more profound level. On the other hand, failing to pay attention to someone's Meta programs can rapidly lead to a catastrophic breakdown in communication and can quickly cause conflict and a misunderstanding of intent.

Rookie Buster

People who operate with similar Meta programs will find that they very quickly create rapport when communicating with one another.

Our Meta programs highlight the processes we use when implementing most of our thinking, and recognizing them provides us with a base understanding of where to begin implementing change.

In a similar way to how our beliefs are formed, we begin creating our Meta programs during our childhood under the influence of our parents and figures of authority, and of our childhood environment. As we develop, our Meta programs develop as well. Our experience changes them, sometimes installing stronger ranges in their influence or in extreme cases turning them inside out and operating them from the opposite side of the scale.

Someone who is "global" (that is, who focuses on the end result and the bigger picture) may choose to become "detailed" (focusing on specific information and tiny details), perhaps as a result of losing a multi-million dollar account due to overlooking some small but crucial detail.

Most of the Meta programs we operate are functioning on an unconscious level. They are not fixed in structure and we do not operate any specific model at any specific time. In fact, as our situations change, so will our Meta models. Sometimes we will subconsciously respond with one, while at other times we may combine various different structures and run them all systematically together.

Everyday Meta programs applied to work and management

We all operate a range of different Meta programs and each one influences our actions and perceptions to varying degrees, as shown on this scale:

Meta program scale

"Away from"   "Towards"

| -9 | -7 | -5 | -3 | -1 | 0 | 1 | 3 | 5 | 7 | 9 |

1. Towards and Away from

People operating a **"Towards"** value program will have tremendous (and sometimes blinkered) focus upon their goals. Their actions are motivated by the perceived benefits and gains behind an objective and their desire to attain it.

Towards people are brilliant at setting themselves goals and targets and are constantly creating new ones to focus on. The downside can be that sometimes these people overlook possible risks and may struggle to complete on tasks, often choosing to move to the new and more exciting.

Rookie Buster

Towards people are brilliant at setting themselves goals and targets.

94   In management a Towards person will be motivated through praise and goal incentives.

Advantages
Positive and optimistic, confident in their approach to work, forward thinking, good social skills, lots of energy and drive.

Disadvantages
May get distracted by having too many bright new goals on the horizon, can have a tendency to make mistakes through their enthusiasm.

People operating an **"Away from"** program are often motivated into action through their perceptions of negatives. They focus their attention on the possibility that things may go wrong, and will often avoid taking on new opportunities due to their wariness of the potential negative outcomes. An Away from person will be motivated into action because they don't want to experience something bad rather than because they want to experience something good.

In management an Away from person will perform better with regular, firm appraisals and stricter management tactics.

Advantages
Good at recognizing potential hazards, spotting errors and risks.

Disadvantages
Will avoid potential opportunities, can be quite negative in their approach to things and over cautious.

Where do you fit on this scale?

2. Options and Procedure

People operating an **"Options"** program will spend their time looking over all the choices available in life. They are generally optimistic in nature and like to consider lots of different options before deciding upon any one idea.

Variety is of great importance to these people, although it can lead to distraction, procrastination and an inability to make a decision. People with Options values are always thinking the grass is greener on the other side.

In management these people respond well to roles that offer plenty of variety and opportunities for providing different working methodologies. However it is worth noting that Options people can struggle to perform repetitive tasks or in any structured environments. Options people can also have a maverick approach to work, so they will happily test the system and may occasionally break the rules.

Advantages
Generally happy in nature, will always be looking for new ways to try things; they perceive multiple choices and will often spot opportunities that others may overlook. Love variety, very creative and crave change.

Disadvantages
They will struggle to complete repetitive tasks, can procrastinate, will avoid making decisions, struggle to focus and are often unsettled.

People operating **"Procedure"** programs need systems, structure and order within their day. Without them they become easily confused and overwhelmed into paralysis. These people are very obedient, enjoy writing lists and are very methodical in their approach to life and its tasks. They are incredibly reliable and will happily focus on repetitive tasks, but they do struggle with change and find it difficult to take on new information and procedures.

In management these people are easy to influence and will often stick within the agreed rules. Procedure people are very reliable, but

96   may struggle to become innovative thinkers and would make terrible sales people. They generally respond well to micro management and an organized, structured environment.

Advantages
Very methodical, enjoy a systematic approach to life. Like to follow rules, very obedient, obliging, very tidy, organized and reliable.

Disadvantages
Easy to unnerve. Can get lost in the procedures and miss the bigger picture; narrow minded, struggle to think for themselves, hate change, not very adaptable, strict, no innovation, And perfectionist.

Where do fit you on this scale?

3. Internal and External

People operating an **"Internal** "program only seek confirmation from within themselves. If someone is internally referenced they will rely upon their own personal judgements before allowing external opinions to influence their decisions or perceptions.

Internal people rely upon their own feelings, senses, thinking and values to gain reassurance that their actions are justified. They will very rarely seek out advice from others. Internal people can be their own harshest critics and their most avid supporters. They can appear to be selfish, aloof and sometimes over confident. In management, these people can prove difficult to influence and will need a strong argument that reflects their values and beliefs before being persuaded into action.

Advantages
Can remain motivated, even in difficult situations. Self reliant. Confident, hard to manipulate.

Disadvantages

Selfish, over critical, unrealistically high standards, difficult to manage, ignore external advice and evidence against internal judgements.

People operating an **"External"** program are constantly seeking external feedback for confirmation of their self worth, deeds, decisions and actions. These people are prone to sheep-like qualities and will always follow the decision of the pack rather than thinking for themselves. Externally focused people can appear needy and often feel insecure within themselves, lacking self assurance.

Rookie Buster

> People operating an "External" program are constantly seeking external feedback for confimation of their self worth.

In management, External people need constant praise and reassurance. They enjoy being presented with all the facts and work best as part of a team, as they are fantastic team players and motivators. If left alone, they may become insecure, demotivated and depressed.

Advantages

Interact well with others, sociable, aware of other people's feelings and motivations, excellent at rapport and provide brilliant customer/client service.

Disadvantages

Always need external reassurance, rely upon external feedback for recognition in order to respond and progress. Often indecisive and can become nervous and quiet in one-to-one situations.

Where do you fit on this scale?

98   4. In time and Through time

People operating an **"In time"** program enjoy living in the moment and have a tendency to ignore tomorrow, focusing upon the immediate experiences of today, the here and now.

Whatever actions they are performing or people they are speaking to in any given moment, their subject will have their complete attention, but once the moment has passed, whatever they were focusing upon is soon lost and forgotten.

In management, In time people are great at achieving the task in hand and can create the impression of giving their customer complete undivided attention and understanding. However, the manager of an In time person would be wise to remember they can be unreliable and it would be worth keeping their tasks to a minimum rather than overloading them. An In time person may be easily distracted and may often arrive late for work, although it will never be personal and their apologies will be sincere.

Advantages
Value the moment, enthusiastic, focused upon the task in hand.

Disadvantages
Struggle to perceive anything beyond the moment. This can lead them to being late for meetings and appointments and struggling even to notice goals, let alone remain focused on them.

Individuals with a **"Through time"** program will spend a lot of their time planning, creating lists and schedules, constantly updating their mental diary. A Through time person is always analysing their next move and the next task, and will be constantly flitting off to prepare for the next event. These people are fantastic timekeepers, but have a tendency to miss the opportunities available to them in the present. This preoccupation with the future can leave others with the impression that they are uninterested, bored or simply have other places to

go and things to attend to, which in some ways is true.

In management a Through time person makes a good administrator or PA, as they are able to remember long lists of things to do, places to go and communications that need addressing. They are not however known for their people skills and may often upset other members of a team, as well as clients and customers.

Advantages

Good organizational and timekeeping skills; forward thinking.

Disadvantages

Can appear bored and uninterested; often poor at rapport.

Where do you fit on this scale?

5. Global and Detail

People with a **"Global"** program will understand situations by focusing upon the bigger picture. These people are good at staying focused by keeping their eye on the eventual objectives, and great at remaining goal focused and selling the eventual dream to customers and clients.

Rookie Buster

People with a "Global" program will understand situations by focusing upon the bigger picture.

Unfortunately these people can struggle to focus on the minute details of a situation and can become easily confused and overwhelmed

100 by the intrinsic information. Give a Global person too much information and they will soon get lost in the detail and will struggle to understand and follow the thread of any conversation.

In management, Global people make good salespeople, as they can
focus their subject's attention upon the larger objectives (shiny car,
rather than weekly payments). They are very good at creating big ideas
and shaping company objectives, but they will struggle to plan their day
or create a detailed business plan and can sometimes end up procrasti-
nating because they struggle to understand what needs tackling first.

Advantages
Good at creating large concept and focusing attention upon the bigger
picture; can often prove to be good motivators.

Disadvantages
Can struggle with detailed information, and can be easily overwhelmed
with too many options or ideas; can struggle to make decisions and
often overlook the finer details.

People with a **"Detail"** program are very focused when it comes to
understanding all the tiny elements of a process and the specifics of a
decision. Detail people enjoy extracting every specific quality from a
conversation and are very good at spotting tiny mistakes and flaws and
at reading the small print.

In management, Detail people make good analysts, accountants or
insurers. They are very particular in their temperament and like everything to be done in a very specific way. They are good at overseeing
company plans, developing strategies and analysing procedures and
effectiveness. They can be perfectionists and can sometimes prove to
be slightly temperamental and can get easily upset about the smaller
things in life.

Advantages
Happy working and studying large amounts of specific details, focused
and persistent, good at spotting mistakes that are often overlooked and
making sense out of chaotic data.

Disadvantages

Can struggle to move beyond the detail and can lose time working through all of the particulars, rather than progressing towards the overall goal. Often seen as pedantic, fickle and unimaginative.

Where do you fit on this scale?

6. Sameness and Difference

People operating a **"Sameness"** model understand new information by comparing to past experiences. They will often stick to methodologies that they have tried, tested and already understand. These people enjoy familiarity and struggle to comprehend any new information as they have no reference system for it. Sameness people love repetition, hate change and once settled in their lives are likely to remain that way permanently.

Rookie Buster

People operating a "Sameness" model understand new information by comparing to past experiences.

In management, Sameness people respond well to familiar environments, consistent expectations, appraisals and micro management, and are happiest when working within a structured and repetitive working environment. These people will generally respond badly to change and will feel insecure or uncomfortable if you decide to move the office furniture around.

Sameness people are extremely reliable and consistent in their working styles, unlikely to put themselves forward for promotion and unlikely ever to leave an organization once established there.

Advantages
Reliable, consistent and happy to do repetitive tasks.

Disadvantages
Stubborn, difficult to influence and unwilling to try new things or perceive new ideas; will resist any changes in the work place.

People operating a "**Difference**" program are always looking for new ways of changing things. Easily bored and constantly unsettled, Difference people love variety and find it very hard to settle on any career choice, management style, goal or even how to take their morning coffee. Difference people are very creative and will always be inventing new ideas and looking for new ways to go about doing things. Difference people hate structure, and struggle to recognize patterns, as their minds can only notice the new and revolutionary, and because of this they quickly disregard anything that is deemed old and has no perceived value.

In management, Difference people tend to be self employed, and they do well working as journalists or as actors, or in any career that offers them constant change. Difference people make good business developers and are best managed with patience, a long leash and a firm steering hand. From a management point of view these people are most successfully influenced by highlighting the variety of experiences on offer within the working day and by guiding their focus to all the new pieces of information they have yet to perceive.

Advantages
Always happy to try new ideas and approaches and to evolve their working style. Enjoy learning and training courses and will happily deal with new products, customers or clients.

Disadvantages
Can be constantly unsettled; will create change for change's sake; lack stability or focus.

Where do you fit on this scale?

What happens when your Meta programs clash with others?

In any environment, communication can break down. Meta programs may sometimes clash, and issues may not be addressed with similar understanding. For example, if someone with a "Through time" orientation begins working alongside an "In time" person, the Through time person will soon become annoyed.

Imagine both parties are working on the same assignment, with the same deadlines and the same scheduled meeting. How long do you think it would take the carefully organized, forever planning Through time person to become frustrated with the focused-on-the-moment In time person? Equally, how long would it be before the In time person became annoyed by the Through time person's constant reference to time? From the In time person's viewpoint, the Through time person obviously has better things to be getting on with and is simply distracting them both from their work with all this talk about something that doesn't matter right now.

These types of conflict can happen within the other Meta programs too. It is difficult to influence the way other people choose to operate their Meta programs, but recognizing them can influence the way you choose to respond and react to them.

You may not be able to change someone else's operating structure, but through the understanding of the Meta programs, you can choose to change the impact other people have upon you, and you can certainly choose to change the scale by which you operate yourself.

Coach's notes

Sliding the scale

1. Spend a couple of minutes looking through your own list of your personal Meta programs and decide whether or not you think they are productive or counter productive in attaining your goals.

2. If you find that they are counter productive, look through the Meta programs and identify the qualities you would like to introduce to alter this behaviour. Write down some ideas of how you can begin introducing these new qualities into your daily life. How will you know when you are finally achieving the results you want?

3. Work towards lowering the scale number of the qualities you find are having a negative impact, and increase and introduce all of the qualities that you want to experience more of – those that you find provide you with a positive impact on your life.

Once you become aware of your own Meta programs, you can choose to uncover which ones are serving you well and which ones aren't. Armed with that information, you can then learn to alter, change or introduce Meta programs that help you to create the results you want.

Go for it! What happens if you are operating a Meta program that is not serving you very well and is actually preventing you from achieving what it is you want? Your Meta programs have developed in response to certain situations over the years, but they are not set in stone. The key is becoming aware. If your personal Meta programs are counterproductive, change your scale slightly and introduce some of the qualities of your desired behaviour. And if you're doing something that you find is not serving your needs – change it.

Notes

Notes

The Meta model was created by Richard Bandler and John Grinder to identify categories of language patterns and gain a deeper under-standing of an individual's experience. Through this chapter you will be taught how to use the Meta model, one of the most powerful verbal tools in business. You will also learn how to spot your own and other's limitations and explore different ways of approaching situations, in turn opening up more choices and options to you. The Meta model will help you to become more efficient and effective in both your profes-sional and personal lives. This will help decrease conflict and mis-understanding and allow you to gain more specific, relevant results.

CHAPTER 7

The Meta model

The Meta model

Language, either written or verbal, provides a medium to allow our complex thoughts, feelings, ideas and experiences to be broken down into a tangible structure for others to interpret. Unfortunately, although our language is powerful it is also flawed, forever unable to capture the entire structure of our thoughts, and it will often fall short of being able to convey the true meaning behind all of our intent.

Rookie Buster

Language will often fall short of being able to convey the true meaning behind all of our intent.

Imagine trying to describe the oceans: a vast amount of water, filled with fish and other sea creatures, and sometimes cold, deep, shallow,

110 warm, depending upon which part of the world you happen to be in. We could write an entire book attempting to explain the oceans and still fail to capture more than a minute percentage of all the tiny details, experiences, knowledge and beauty actually contained within them.

It is common procedure for most organizations to have a written company identity, the business literature stating "who are we" on the company website. The principal reason for this summary is to provide potential clients and employees with a deeper insight into the company as a whole – its culture, people, management, products, objectives and successes.

Unfortunately, no matter how many paragraphs the organization devotes to this, it is still nothing more than a mere summary, a selective, generalized and distorted view of all the information that is actually available, made up of the tiny events that actually occur within the corporate walls on a daily basis.

This doesn't make what has been written about the company any the less true, but it just means that the information is incomplete, only a small fragment of all the vast amount of information available.

One of the most powerful influencing tools we have is our language, but it is important to recognize that it has massive limitations, and although it provides us with an outlet for our thoughts, it can never fully deconstruct, capture or portray the entire span of our meanings, feelings, ideas, experience and understanding.

Rookie Buster

One of the most powerful influencing tools we have is our language.

The Meta model provides us with a methodology that gives us access to the deep structure operating behind our language, creating the opportunity to gain insight and clarity into the specific meaning behind our words.

We have already mentioned that when our minds take on any information, it all has to be filtered through our belief and value structures, resulting in only a small percentage of that information actually getting through.

A similar thing happens when we begin communicating and interacting with one another. We have so many structures within our minds, creating our internal reality, that for even basic communication to occur with one another, we must summarize and filter information down, turning it into more tangible structures.

Understanding an individual's Meta models brings us closer to understanding their true experience of reality. If we understand what is actually going on within someone else's head, the thoughts that are driving them, the motivation and the actual meaning behind the words they say, it becomes easier for us to answer their genuine questions and respond with the appropriate behaviour or the relevant information, rather than guessing at what they are saying and often getting it wrong.

Rookie Buster

If we understand what is actually going on within someone else's head, it becomes easier for us to answer their genuine questions and respond with the appropriate behaviour.

Through their studies, Bandler and Grinder noticed that people process language in three distinct ways: deletion, distortion and generalization.

By applying these filtering processes to our language, we allow our thoughts and our communication of these thoughts to become more manageable, enabling our mind to convey our meaning without the intent getting lost within rambling and irrelevant detail.

The language we use every day is known as our *surface structure*. This means that the actual words being used are only a surface

112 representation of the actual, deeper meaning contained within our thoughts. This deeper meaning (the intent) behind our language is known as *the deeper structure* or *higher order structure* of language. Uncovering this deeper meaning (the true intent) behind the words people are using can provide us with the key that unlocks the specific information we need in order to tune into another person's honest perspective and allow us to communicate with them at a higher level than we would normally.

The Meta model teaches us how to gather more effective information from the language that we and others use. By asking the right questions we can uncover the hidden meaning behind deletion, distortion and generalization and clarify the truth behind what we are actually meaning, not just what we are saying.

Deletion

Deletion occurs when you are not giving the whole story and you are editing out specifics from the sentence. When deletion occurs in our language it leaves the recipient in a position where they have to fill in the gaps themselves, and almost make it up. Have you ever noticed yourself finishing someone else's sentence before they have had a chance to do it themselves? And when you did that, were you actually able to read the mind of the other person or did you simply fill in the blanks with your own opinion of the perceived conversation?

Because there is so much information bombarding our senses both internally and externally, in order to save us time and to prevent our minds from becoming overwhelmed with any unnecessary data, our subconscious has a tendency to delete anything it deems to be irrelevant. This often results in our conscious mind being aware only of the specific details that relate to our belief structures and values, often overlooking more productive data that is also available.

Deletion is a valuable screening tool, but because it can perceive only the information it expects to see, sometimes the negative effect can be that it also leads us into unrealistic and sometimes unhelpful and restrictive perceptions.

For example, when you gain feedback from your quarterly appraisal, you may subconsciously delete any negative feedback that you believed didn't accurately reflect how you personally viewed your own performance.

Or when listening to a presentation, you may find yourself deleting any information that doesn't resonate with your current interest, choosing instead to daydream about other matters of more personal importance. Have you ever walked out after a lecture and wondered what exactly had been said?

Or have you ever found yourself rejecting a compliment because it didn't mirror with what you believed to be true?

Deletion doesn't occur only in our input of information. We delete our language all the time, subconsciously choosing not to use words in order to save time and energy for the person speaking. It's a little similar to the texting culture we have developed, deleting characters to save space and time. You becomes "u" and later becomes "l8r". And "lol" stands for laugh out loud, which is fine if you understand the language of text, but if not, you could be left struggling to interpret it.

Deletion is time saving, but it also has a tendency to limit our thinking and restrict the way in which we perceive the world. Compliments often go unheard, feedback remains unacknowledged and opportunities are unrecognized.

Rookie Buster

Deletion is time saving, but it also has a tendency to limit our thinking and restrict the way in which we perceive the world.

114 Examples of deletion in language

Simple deletions about things
"It's harder than I thought," or "That was nice!" (What?)
Specific objects or things are often replaced by "this", "that" or "it".
Deletions about people
"He made it happen," or "They thought it was a good idea." (Who?)
Deletions about how events happened
"I sold it to him." (What to who? And how?)

Deletions such as these often remove necessary information behind what is actually being said.

How the Meta model clarifies

The Meta model provides questions to gather more specific information and clarify the deeper structure of the language being used:

- Who, what, when, how?
- What specifically?
- What exactly?

With simple deletions (What?), say "What was harder than you thought?" or "What was nice?"

With deletions about people (Who?), say "Who specifically?" ("Who specifically made it happen?" or "Who thought it was a good idea?")

With deletions about how events happened (How?), you can ask questions beginning with "How?" or "How exactly?" ("How exactly did you sell it to him?")

Generalization

Generalization occurs when one experience is linked to another for understanding. Our mind takes the meaning from one experience, object or idea and then links this understanding and coded pattern to another separate experience, object or idea, basically transferring one conclusion on to another reference point.

Generalizations provide our subconscious mind with a quick method of structuring the world and our experiences into an easily accessible cognitive map, for example if the rules of playing baseball are transferred into understanding how to learn tennis. Both sports involve a sort of bat and ball, use similar coordination and motor skills and apply similar basic principles.

Saying that "Everyone in HR is rubbish" demonstrates how the mind has generalized the title and understanding of HR to anybody unfortunate enough to have a job within HR. In that statement *all* the people in Human Resources have just been tarred with the same brush, probably merely because at some point someone has maybe had a bad experience with one or two relatively incompetent HR people.

Through generalization you can apply existing understanding on to another subject, making slight alterations to the basic program if necessary, often using your past to understand your future, thereby saving your subconscious valuable processing time.

Rookie Buster

Through generalization you can apply existing understanding on to another subject.

The downside to relying upon our past to understand our present and our future, the new and the unexperienced, is that sometimes new, potentially interesting or relevant details are overlooked and missed. If your mind happens to perceive X to be like Y, it then can go on to assume that X therefore must also have the same or a similar meaning to Y. This assumption then leads the subconscious to automatically respond to X as if it was in fact Y, even though X is a whole new subject and letter.

These assumptions can lead to devaluing ideas, experiences, perceived gestures and wonderful opportunities. Because generalization

116   often oversimplifies things, it can sometimes leave very little room for any new arguments or new thinking to be considered.

Examples of generalization in language

All, always, never, everyone, everything:
- "All recruitment staff are vultures."
- "I never do well in interviews."
- "Everything I do turns out badly."

Overcoming generalization can be achieved by questioning the specifics behind our words:
- "Do *all* people act this way?"
- "What happens if you do?"
- "What happens if you don't?"
- "Just imagine you could, what then?"
- "What is possible?"
- "What is impossible?"

Distortion

Distortion is a misinterpretation of information and it occurs when we change and alter the actual meaning behind communication and distort it into something else. The new structure is usually something more reflective of our own personal belief system.

We are continuously manipulating the information available in reality and distorting it into reflecting what we believe to be true, rather than considering the potential options of its actual meaning. When we allow ourselves to become completely focused upon something that we truly believe is right, we can often blind ourselves into ignoring and changing any evidence that may possibly

state otherwise. Distortion is a result of our perceptions and beliefs coming together.

Rookie Buster

Distortion is a result of our perceptions and beliefs coming together.

We focus our attention upon the information that backs up our reality and our own personal points of interest on our cognitive map, because our conscious can only comprehend a limited amount of information. Any new information available to our subconscious mind that our beliefs deem irrelevant will simply be ignored. Distortion is very rarely a conscious act, and often people tend not to realize that what they perceive isn't always actually the truth.

Distortion can also be a brilliant creative tool and can allow our mind to change things so as to perceive them in new lights and from different angles. By distorting our perceptions on things we can create new realities, dreams and brilliant inventions. However when we consciously allow ourselves to distort reality, we have to be very careful that we are choosing to create something made of dreams rather than of nightmares.

What if?

Distortion is often applied with mind reading, and is something we do when we are trying to interpret another person's intention. But it is important to recognize that because everyone's perceptions and understanding of reality is so different, we can never know what someone else is thinking exactly or truly understand the intention behind their words, unless we choose to ask them.

Trying to view someone else's map through our own perception

118 will distort the reality immensely, and will taint the meaning behind their words and actions. Negative distortions blended with mind reading can have very debilitating effects. To make any judgement on or draw any conclusion from someone else's actions or deeds involves a process of evaluation based upon the available evidence.

Rookie Buster

To make any judgement on or draw any conclusion from someone else's actions or deeds involves a process of evaluation based upon the available evidence.

It is important that we are careful that we gather enough evidence to view the case properly and even then, make sure we are viewing that information from every possible light.

Examples of distortion in language

- "I don't know."
- "You never say that."
- "I know they think I'm no good."
- "It must be my fault."
- "I know that they will think this is great."

Overcoming distortion can be achieved by questioning the specifics behind our words:

- "Who (or what) says?"
- "How do you know?"
- "What makes that mean this?"

Coach's notes

Practising the Meta model

1. Next time you are speaking with a client or a colleague, begin actively listening to their language and attempt to spot their distortions, generalizations and deletions. Listen to the actual words they are using. Try and identify what it is they are not actually saying.

2. Once you have identified their distortions, generalizations and deletions, begin to challenge and question them. What is it they specifically want, what are their actual motivating factors and what are they expecting you to deliver them and how?

3. Start learning how to ask the right questions. How do they know, and what evidence are they backing this conclusion up with?

But before any communication can begin, always remember to establish rapport first!

Go for it! The Meta model is a valuable tool to apply in business, as it allows you to understand and use language in a way that clarifies people's actual meaning. What do they want, what are their motivating factors, and what are they expecting from you? Through the Meta model we can understand other people's true objectives, clarify meaning and gain understanding into our own limiting thought processes. By clarifying all the details within a situation we get to perceive and open ourselves up to all the available choices.

Notes

Because our minds work within a methodology that is very systematic and streamlined, it is often seeking new ways of linking one piece of information to another, searching out any perceived similarities between subjects and creating relationships of understanding between them. In this chapter we will learn how to manipulate and utilize the influential effects of language, creating words that will inspire, influence and create impact upon any targeted audience.

CHAPTER 8

Once upon a something ...

Stories, fables and metaphors

What stories can do

Stories and metaphors are a simple yet powerful way of demonstrating new ideas, providing the mind with deeper insight and meaning. Stories are conveyed through motivational anecdotes, seamlessly linking powerful and emotive words to what might otherwise have been a mere lifeless instruction. Presentations, talks, interviews and teachings can all be greatly improved by adding the odd metaphor or anecdote.

Rookie Buster

Stories and metaphors are a simple yet powerful way of demonstrating new ideas, providing the mind with deeper insight and meaning.

124   Stories with a hidden meaning captured within rhythm, rhyme, adventure and creation have been used throughout the centuries to pass on the tales and understanding of the past. For centuries clans and tribes have relied upon stories to pass on the history and wisdom of the past generations. Wandering minstrels used stories and rhyme to spread current news as well as propaganda, while religious books contain stories of intent and spiritual understanding.

We can find many examples of times when stories have been used to influence our perceptions and connect to our experiences, memories and emotions.

Stories are also fantastic for creating good business communication across genres and cultures. They can illustrate difficult new points, introduce new ideas and provide information offering solutions to difficult problems, changing ideals, influencing moods and offering a new perception of the list of choices available to our behaviour.

Rookie Buster

Stories are also fantastic for creating good business communication across genres and cultures.

Stories can be used to create rapport and to demonstrate common ground in experience or ideals. They can introduce the new and unknown by providing a reference map of understanding, and they can take an intent or make a point and convey it in a manner that is more acceptable to the subconscious mind.

Stories stir imagination and emotions, influencing the entire representational system in a way that creates strong connections within the mind, linking the words to deeper understanding.

How stories free the subconscious mind 125

Stories can influence our belief structures and open the door to new possibilities.

Your subconscious is always looking for ways to sort and code its information, searching out links and patterns and matching new information to old for a more streamlined understanding.

Stories engage both the left and right hand sides of the brain. The right side provides the creativity, the imagination and the story – the life to our tale – while the left side listens to the words and spots the logic, understanding the patterns and sequential information constructing the tale.

Stories have a brilliant way of engaging and distracting our conscious mind, freeing the subconscious to compare, sort, match and mirror with the information being offered. Because this new information is not perceived as a threat to our belief system, it is simply offered up as new information that the subconscious mind can sort through and gain new solutions, choices or ideals from.

Testimonials tell stories too

Testimonials and case studies in business are versions of storytelling; they recount information in an effective way that creates trust and demonstrates knowledge and success to your clients. "I found 'Business X' provided us with a service that was reliable and professional. The staff were friendly and knew immediately how to provide my company with the effective solution to our problem. We will certainly be using them again." (Testimonial by Client Z.)

Rookie Buster

Testimonials and case studies in business are versions of storytelling.

126   This testimonial takes an idea (that Business X is good) and makes it real, or at least provides the possibility that it *could* be real (because Client Z says so).

By being presented with an example of Business X's abilities, we are given apparent proof that a currently unknown idea or product (Business X) actually exists, as we now have some tangible evidence (the testimonial) that our mind can relate to, evaluate and create a conclusion from.

A potential buyer reading the statement would be able to link the testimonial from Client Z to the currently unknown Business X and create a probable conclusion that Business X is good at what it does (providing solutions), because Client Z has said so.

The route to understanding

To understand anything, whether words, objects, feelings or sounds, your brain has to recreate the experience first within the mind, reliving it and resonating with it before eventually arriving at a conclusion of understanding.

Imagine you were going to try and explain what emails were to your elderly and technologically naive grandmother. How would you set about it?

You might say something like: "An email is similar to a handwritten letter, but instead of using paper and pen, we type the letter on a computer and then use something called the internet to deliver it for us. The internet is like the postal system, except it doesn't need a stamp, and instead of relying upon a postman to deliver our mail, the computer does it for us. It's a much more effective way of communicating, as it's much faster and much more reliable than our postal system is."

By using the words "like" and "similar", you create connections between the two ideas that your grandmother's mind can quickly spot, and then create a relationship of understanding.

Stories don't have to begin with "once upon a time". Any time you come back from a hard day at the office and retell the day's events to your nearest and dearest, you are effectively storytelling – you are recounting the events of the day in a way that you know your audience will understand and resonate with. If you want your tale to have more impact, then you may add a bit of humour or drama. The more unusual the contents of a tale, the more likely it is to stand out within the sub-conscious, and the more likely people are to remember it.

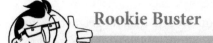

Rookie Buster

Stories don't have to begin with "once upon a time".

All our stories contain the following vital ingredients:
- There is always a hero, a main character.
- There is always a villain or an obstacle influencing the tale.
- Other secondary characters, friends, co-workers, etc.
- The story has a plot, with a beginning, a middle and an end.
- An objective to the tale, a purpose.
- To finish off with, a conclusion.

Here's an example:

"[Beginning] We had our reviews [purpose] at work yesterday. I [the hero] can't believe how nervous I was, sitting at my desk, watching as my colleagues [secondary characters] sloped off one by one into the meeting room, feet dragging across the carpet before disappearing inside.

"I felt sick waiting for my turn, imagining all the terrible things that my boss [the villain] might say, all my flaws he might choose to point out.

"Before I knew it, the minutes had flown by and it was my turn to head towards the meeting room [middle of tale]. My heart began to race and my hands became clammy. I hoped I wouldn't have to shake my boss's hand.

"As I sat down, I saw that he was smiling. He leaned back in his chair and told me this would be an easy review to give, as he thought the work I had been doing so far was great [end of tale]. I immediately relaxed and began wondering what on earth it was I had been worried about [conclusion]."

Exercise: Using storytelling to get your message across

Think of a purpose or a message you would like to get across to someone else. Maybe you are going for an interview and you need to demonstrate your past working experiences to your interviewers.

Write down:

1. Who is the main character in this tale (you, for example)?
2. What is the purpose of your story, the message you want to get across? (For example, "I am great and can do this job.")
3. Who is the villain or what is the obstacle in the tale? (For instance, what problem did you solve that demonstrates your purpose?)
4. What is your plot, and what are the beginning, middle and end of your story? (For example, in your previous job [beginning], you were handling these objectives [middle] and the client thought you were great [the end].)
5. What is your conclusion? (For example, if they employ you they will gain all of these benefits because you can do X, Y and Z.)

If you really want to build trust from your

employer, provide a testimonial from a previous employer or client   129
(often known as references).

Metaphors

Metaphors provide us with a wonderful tool for taking the unknown
and making it accessible. They enable us to effectively communicate
our intended messages or meanings in a way that the subconscious
mind finds easy to accept and understand.

Rookie Buster

Metaphors provide us with a wonderful tool for taking
the unknown and making it accessible.

All of our thoughts are coded within our mind and stored away as
referential patterns. Our mind uses this library of archived experience
to refer back to and compare new information against, therefore allowing it always to remain abreast of the constantly changing world around
us.

Our subconscious mind does not like the unknown, and to understand any new piece of information it must rely upon our previously
collected and patterned resources and experiences to provide any new
experiences, ideas or concepts with relevant insight and meaning.

It is through your previous patterned experiences that your mind is
able to forge new relationships with your new experiences and by that
means to understand them. One of your subconscious mind's natural
functions is to recognize similarities and relationships between information, acknowledging and linking these relationships back to any
previously gained understanding.

Metaphors are a beautiful way of demonstrating the specific
meaning behind our language. They also contain the immense power

130   of being able to communicate meaning in a manner that is effective and often emotive, as they illustrate pictures in a way that simple language cannot. They allow the brain to make comparisons and connect words that would normally remain unrelated, but that when used in a different way can effectively demonstrate a point:

- "The office was a sea of silence."
- "Working in a telesales environment is like working in a battery farm."

Rookie Buster

Metaphors are a beautiful way of demonstrating the specific meaning behind our language.

Metaphors allow the listener to make paralleled conclusions from the information, relating it to their own understanding, gaining a new perspective and providing an emotive response that can motivate, open up new possibilities or highlight new perspectives.

NLP often uses metaphors to lead someone from one reality or context into another, as they are a wonderful way of introducing new concepts while keeping the intent behind your words tangible and relevant to the listener. Using them provides understanding by linking new ideas to the audience's way of thinking.

Metaphors can also be a great way to gain access into someone's perceived way of thinking. By discussing ideas metaphorically, and using their reality, you can often help people perceive new solutions to their problems.

Using metaphor to get your message across

PERSON A: Walking into that interview is going to feel as though I'm walking into the lions' den.

PERSON B: If that case you've got to be prepared. What do you need to do to tame their killer focus on you?

PERSON A: Maybe I could distract them with my charm or examples of my past experience?

PERSON B: Okay. Well, considering you really want this job, and these interviewing lions are the only obstacle currently in your way, while you're distracting them, how will you then turn this situation around so you change from being the hunted to the hunter?

PERSON A: While I distract them with stories of my experience, I could also weave into the tale my extensive knowledge, my acknowledgements and examples of what they would gain by having me on board.

PERSON B: Do you think by doing this you could turn these lions into pussycats and have them eating out of your hand?

PERSON A: I'm not sure about that, but it would be good if I could leave them purring when they thought about me in this role.

Metaphors are wonderful ways of exploring a situation differently, sometimes providing solutions that may not have been perceived otherwise. And metaphors can make a potentially intimidating situation appear less so, when qualities are altered slightly.

Rookie Buster

Metaphors can make a potentially intimidating situation appear less so.

132 *Storytelling at work*

Stories are a fantastic tool for creating impact within communication. But all stories develop and change over time, so learn to re-use the elements of your tale in a way that allows you to alter and manipulate its parts so that they can evolve into the structure that is most suitable for the purpose.

A well-told story can capture the imagination and subconscious of an entire audience. And a well-told story remains long after the storyteller is forgotten.

You can use storytelling at work to:

- Help your team look at new opportunities and choices.
- Introduce new concepts, products and training.
- Improve your interview or presentation techniques.
- Convey the values of the organization.

Reframing

The creative flair we apply to our stories can also be used to alter the way in which we perceive the meaning or the impact of certain information. This is called "reframing", and the ability to reframe is the ability to change your perceptions to view something from a different angle in a way that creates a new meaning.

For example, do you see the glass as half full or half empty? The same glass containing exactly the same amount of liquid can take on two different and almost opposite meanings depending on how you choose to view it:

- Glass half full – positive.
- Glass half empty – negative.

Imagine you're at work and all the computers have crashed and taken the company off line for a couple of hours, so nobody can access the information they need to continue their daily activities.

This can be viewed as a disaster, or you can choose to look at it as an opportunity to take a couple of hours to discuss that new company training you just haven't had time to get around to before.   133

Is a lack of promotion a sign you're no good at your job, or an opportunity to seek more inspiring employment?

Is an interview something to fear, or an opportunity to embrace?

Everything has more than one perception if you actively choose to look at it from another angle.

Rookie Buster

Everything has more than one perception if you actively choose to look at it from another angle.

Exercise: 6-step reframing

1. *What behaviour do you want to change?*
"I want to be able to do ABC, but I always end up doing XYZ, or LMN stops me."

Acknowledging that your subconscious only works in the positive, remember it has been operating this behaviour because of a perceived positive intention. Spend a brief moment allowing yourself to recognize and thank your subconscious for looking after you.

2. *Ask your subconscious to acknowledge the part of your mind responsible for this behaviour.*
Become aware of all of your senses, internal feelings, sights, sounds and sensations. Now, with this awareness, ask yourself internally, "Will the part responsible for XYZ behaviour come forward and communicate with me now?"

You will notice something change within you, as your subconscious responds (it may feel similar to your intuition). Keep practising this until you have a strong, established signal.

134   *3. Now, with your response established, you want to move the positive intent out from the unwanted behaviour.*

Ask yourself internally, "Will the part responsible for this XYZ behaviour become aware of the intent driving it, what is it trying to achieve?"

You should notice a "yes" response; you may even become consciously aware of the intent driving the function. If you get a "no", don't worry: you don't have to become aware for the habit to change, but do then ask, "Is the part responsible for this XYZ behaviour happy to move the intent anyway?"

If you still get a "no", then maybe you need to clarify your signals again.

4. We now want the subconscious to create new ways of addressing this intent.

Ask your subconscious, "Can the creative part of my mind find five different ways of accomplishing this intent through other more productive behaviours?"

Notice your response.

Because our mind operates on patterns and similarities, our subconscious recognizes the structures in our intent and can look through our internal library of existing behavioural strategies to find alternative outlets for it by matching it across to similar structures. Once our intent is linked to other similar structures, it can then let go of the unwanted behaviour as it now has alternative options for achieving its desired response.

5. Once your creative mind has uncovered (subconsciously – you may not be consciously aware of this) alternative behavioural options for your intent, you can then ask your subconscious to switch the intent across to these new behaviours.

Ask your subconscious, "Can the creative part of my mind now move the intent behind XYZ into the five newly identified options?"

Notice your response.

If you get a "no", ask your subconscious, "Does any other part of me object to these new choices?"

Notice your response.

If you get a "yes", then go back to Step 4 and ask your subconscious   135
to come up with some more alternative choices.

6. *Once the intent has been removed, you want to ask your subconscious to agree to let go of the unwanted behaviour and instead operate one of your new five options.*
Ask your subconscious, "Is the part of my mind responsible for XYZ happy to let go of this behaviour?"

Notice your response.

If you get a "no", go back to Step 2 and repeat the process again.

If you get a "yes", ask your subconscious, "Is the part of my mind that was responsible for XYZ now happy to run these new behaviours instead?"

Notice your response.

If you get a "no", go back to Step 2.

If you get a "yes", congratulations! You have now successfully reframed your behaviour.

Becoming the storyteller

A useful tool for anyone to have is a small repertoire of stories that can be utilized within various situations throughout your life.

1. Spend some time identifying situations in your life in which it could be appropriate and even helpful to use metaphorical stories. For example:
    - Sales pep talk.
    - Explaining your company's profile to clients.
    - Explaining to your children what it is you do for a living.
2. Draft out the contents of your story. What is its objective, what is its conclusion, who is your audience, what points do you need to get across?
3. Using the framework highlighted earlier in this chapter, create the framework of your story to capture all of your details and important qualities.
4. Once you have written your story, re-read it and practise reading your script out loud until you have learned its main contents off by heart.
5. Practise! Begin introducing your tales into your chosen situations. How well do they work? Are there any elements you need to adjust? Any qualities that may need adding or editing? The more you practise, the better you will become.

By having a couple of well-chosen pre-prepared scripts, you will find that no matter what your situation, or how nervous you may find you are feeling, you can always rely on your subconscious mind to provide you with one of your specific scripts at will. Which means you will always have something useful to say, even in those nightmare situations when your conscious mind has abandoned you and gone completely blank!

Go for it! Stories and metaphors can shed a new light of understanding upon your words. They can help your presentations gain impact and can leave your message imprinted upon your client's mind, long after you have gone.

Remember, everything is perception. An event, communication, situation or behaviour may have more than one meaning or more than one purpose.

By reframing the intent driving your actions, you may find you can change them from unwanted behaviours into useful ones.

138 Notes

Notes

We all have experienced times within our lives when we have truly performed to the best of our abilities, and when everything has simply flowed into place. Imagine the positive impact you could have on your life if you could tap into that high performance state at will. The aim of this chapter is to introduce some of the more influential aspects of NLP. You will learn about Milton Erickson, one of the greatest hypno-therapists of all time and a founding inspiration behind a lot of the NLP models. You will learn how vague language can produce influen-tial effects upon its listeners, creating deeper levels of rapport and communication. By the end of this chapter you will understand how to influence and recognize your internal states and will know how to access the tools required to influence and direct not only your own behaviour but that of others as well.

CHAPTER 9

The way of influence

The Milton model, language and anchoring

The Milton model is the reflective counterpart to the Meta model, and was named in tribute to the man responsible for its inspiration, Milton Erickson.

In 1974, Bandler and Grinder worked with the brilliant hypnotherapist and teacher Dr Milton H. Erickson, modelling his successful approach and methodologies within his chosen field of clinical hypnosis. By that time, Erickson's work in "change therapy" had won him worldwide recognition as one of the most influential hypnotherapists of all time.

Erickson's unique hypnotic style effortlessly guided his patients towards achieving their own internal trance state. Using his subtle observations of non-verbal behaviour and artful implementation of vague language, Milton allowed his subjects to subconsciously uncover their own positive internal resources, leading their minds into providing the solutions required to begin making the appropriate changes in their behaviour.

142   Erickson's approach was to pace his patient's personal reality, understanding that the only way anyone can begin effectively influencing someone else is through an established foundation of trust. This meant being flexible within his own behaviour. He knew that in order for his intent to become properly understood, and for his communication to be truly effective, he had first to join his patients within their own perceived reality, resulting in an extremely permissive hypnotic approach, which began by acknowledging his patient's own neurological "map of the world".

Erickson's use of "vague" language patterns steered his patients towards interpreting his communication in a manner that was relevant to their own perceptions and reflected their own understanding. This led to instant rapport and positive, often inspirational therapy results.

Our minds are always seeking a way to make sense of the world and the communication within it. Our logical mind has a great capacity for organizing any perceived information in a manner that always provides relevant understanding. Even if communication is incredibly vague and none too specific, our minds will still quickly fill in any apparent gaps with our own deemed appropriate interpretation.

Rookie Buster

Our minds are always seeking a way to make sense of the world and the communication within it.

Exercise: Vague language

Ask a friend or colleague to read the previous chapter. Then both of you read the statement below and write down your own personal interpretations of it.

"Once you have finished reading the above chapter, you may find yourself thinking about the new insights you have learned or thinking about how you will begin applying your new understanding into your life."

As you read this paragraph, you will find it is made up of statements, questions and judgements that are without any specific direction or intention.

- Which paragraph?
- Thinking specifically about what?
- What sort of thoughts?
- What exact insight?
- Which words?
- Are you learning and thinking about insight or just applying it?
- Which is it or does it mean both?
- How are you applying it?
- What understanding and which part of your life?

You have to decide and assign all the meanings to the words yourself, which forces your mind to go internally and think about how, why and which elements of the statement are true, potentially relevant and appropriate to you.

Now both of you compare your answers.

You will notice that you have both found a way of responding appropriately to the statement, but the interesting question now is: Are the responses the same, or have you each chosen to interpret the same statement slightly differently?

The differences between the two

The Milton model is basically the Meta model in reverse. It utilizes the same basic patterns as the Meta model, but it applies them in an opposite context. The Meta model forces our mind to go externally,

144   bringing the specific structure and meaning behind our communicated language into our conscious awareness.

The Milton model forces our mind to go internally, and allows our subconscious to search within our own internal resources to gain a more general and relevant understanding from the communicated language.

Pacing

Erickson was a natural when it came to building rapport with his patients. A lot of his rapport came from his constant communicative pacing, both verbal and non verbal (see Chapter 5 on rapport), and he believed that the only reason why someone would put up any resistance to you would be because of lack of established rapport.

Pacing someone's reality is easy to do, and can be something you incorporate into your everyday conversation. To begin pacing someone, you simply need to tune in to their perceived reality, and this can be begun by altering their conscious focus on to a mutual reality (five, seven or nine pieces of conscious attention):

"As you sit on your plastic chairs [pace] and listen to my presentation [pace], imagine [lead] …"

"Since it's late in the afternoon [pace] and it's already starting to get dark [pace], I appreciate you may feel a certain way [vague statement] about speaking to me [pace] on the phone right now, so I'll get to the reason behind why it's important I speak with you …"

You can never truly know what someone else is thinking, but you can control elements of their conscious awareness. This does not mean you are controlling what they are thinking, but simply that you are able to draw their limited focus of attention on to something you can both mutually perceive, creating common ground and the foundations upon which to begin building rapport.

Rookie Buster

> You can never truly know what someone else is thinking, but you can control elements of their conscious awareness.

Vagueness

The Milton model specializes in vagueness, and unlike the Meta model is crammed with deletions, distortion and generalizations. The Milton model forces its listener to actively participate in the communication, searching their own previously collected experiences to understand and attract internal meaning to the words being communicated. This turns the communication into a very personal dialogue, with understanding occurring on a very personal level. The Milton model plays to all our personal belief structures, values and perceptions and leads any analysis of their effectiveness to come from within.

Vague language provides an outline for our thoughts, but doesn't specify the detail. Once mastered it can be a useful and influential tool.

Nominalizations

"Nominalizations" are an NLP term for abstract nouns. They are very effective for deleting specific information out of language and are useful to incorporate into your vague statements. Examples are:

- Fear.
- Love.
- Relationship.
- Happiness.
- Shattered.
- Rubbish.
- Useless.
- Understanding.
- Language.
- Aspirations.

These words were previously verbs ("to be frightened") and have been turned into nouns ("fear"), and they are very hard to define specifically, as everyone's personal interpretation and understanding of them can be different.

Unspecified verbs
These are verbs that have no specific meaning and again lead the listener to seek out and attach their own personal meaning. Examples are:
- Communicate.
- Experience.
- Learning.
- Search.
- Think
- Imagine.

Generalized nouns
These exist when the collection of information behind the word has been left out. Examples are:
- They.
- People.
- Colleagues.
- Changes.
- Clients.

Judgements and comparisons
Judgements and comparisons are also good to use if you want to make a statement that you do not want to be questioned. For example:

"That car is like your tie [comparison] in the way it creates an impression [judgement]. Imagine the statement and impression you will be making to your clients when you turn up in this car [judgement], similar to the statement you make with your tie, a perfect reflection [comparison]."

Although if you are making a judging statement like this, do calibrate first whether or not your listener actually likes their tie!

Universal quantifiers

Universal quantifiers are great for adding weight to your argument. For example:

- *"Everyone* in the office thinks this is a brilliant idea."
- "As a company we think it's important *always* to deliver the highest standard possible, to *every one* of our clients."

"That's right"

"That's right" are two magical words to use in influential language. We are not stating exactly what is right, but we can use these words to agree, confirm and maintain our rapport within someone else's reality.

Tag questions

Tag questions are used to invite agreement from your subject. They can help distract the conscious mind and allow the tag question to go directly to the unconscious mind. For example:

- "It makes perfect sense, doesn't it?"
- "You can understand why this product is a bestseller, can't you?"
- "You can imagine how, with my relevant experience, I would be a perfect fit for this role, can't you?"

Double blinds

Double blinds lead your subject to believing they have options and choices, although these are in fact very limited. They present an idea in a manner that allows your subject to feel that they have a choice in the decision. Using a double blind is a good way of managing someone's behaviour without consciously making them feel manipulated. For example:

- "Do you want to ring the client before or after your lunch break?" (The command is that they will ring the client; the choice is when.)
- "Would you prefer to sign the contract now, or shall we do it after we've looked around the property?"

148

Rookie Buster

Using a double blind is a good way of managing someone's behaviour without consciously making them feel manipulated.

Embedded commands

These are sentences instructing the focus of the subconscious mind, without the conscious mind's logical interference. Most embedded commands are delivered with a change in vocal tonality or pace: "I'm not sure at which point of this conversation you will choose to *meet my client*, but I will go through all the points and we'll see which ones *will match your own requirements*."

Vagueness in language is an incredibly important influencing tool, as it permits our listeners to create and personalize the meaning behind our words. This internal approach to our communication will often prevent the listener's conscious mind from blocking or over-analysing the intent behind our communication, and it also provides the listener with the opportunity of finding the most suitable and appropriate meaning and understanding from within our words.

It is very important that you remember that with influence comes responsibility – so always ensure that all of your communication begins by respecting another person's realities, beliefs and values!

It's a cliché but still an appropriate one: "Always treat others in the way you yourself would wish to be treated."

States

A lot of our responses and interactions with reality are a result of our emotional frame of mind at the time. These mindsets are known in NLP as "states".

Most of our directional behaviour can be influenced through our states. When we feel happy, we are more likely to filter our information to reflect our perception of this state, and under these conditions decisions will become more impulsive, we feel luckier, we will often overlook small negative details and we will generally respond with a more positive, open and proactive approach to life. When we feel in a sad or angry state, again our perceptual filters become influential in the way we then look at and react to life, and our new expectations also inevitably become reality.

Milton Erickson recognized the importance of states when it came to influencing his patients into positively altering their behaviour.

It is easier to persuade your client to sign a multi-million dollar contract when they are in a happy state and feeling optimistic about life. You are more likely to tackle that 10,000-word proposal when your state is motivated, focused and excited about the idea you're proposing.

Rookie Buster

It is easier to persuade your client to sign a multi-million dollar contract when they are in a happy state and feeling optimistic about life.

Mastering how to influence state change both within yourself and within others is a key influential tool that will have a massive impact upon your work, personal and social life.

Since our emotional states are a result of the thoughts that we are thinking, our external perceptions and our internal thought processes, we can actively influence our states by simply manipulating our thoughts.

Exercise: Altering your state

Remember a time when you've felt extremely happy. It doesn't matter what this memory is, whether it is real or imagined, with friends or on your own, as long as the thought makes you smile.

Think for a couple of minutes about this memory. Imagine all the qualities of it. What do you see, hear and feel?

Allow yourself to truly associate with this memory for a couple of minutes, then break state and become aware of reality once more. ("Breaking state" is an NLP term for when you choose to alter your current state and focus of mind and change into a more neutral state. This can be done by simply shaking your body about a bit, moving your arms or shifting your physical position.)

Every time we daydream, play make-believe, watch TV, read a fictional book or just socialize with our friends, we are actively altering our emotional states.

Learning how to alter or create different states on command helps us to choose how and in which direction we wish to direct our behaviour.

Elicitation and the calibration of others

In NLP, the process of understanding someone's state in order to influence and change it is known as "elicitation". "Calibration" occurs when we accurately observe another person's non-verbal signals.

When we are experiencing a specific state, both our mind and body respond at the same time. Our gestures change, our physiology, tonality and even the submodalities within our internal representational system (hearing, seeing, feelings) will begin to alter.

This is useful to remember when you are interacting with others. The only way we can gain any insight into how our communication is being interpreted is by eliciting someone's response to it. Remember: the meaning behind your communication is the response you get. And by learning to recognize another person's state, we can gain the information that allows us to communicate more effectively.

Rookie Buster

The meaning behind your communication is the response you get.

Imagine walking into your boss's office with the intent of asking him for a pay rise and then noticing that he was scowling, his arms were folded and his voice was stern and lifeless. You would probably decide that now wasn't the best moment to approach him and that maybe it would be sensible to leave it to a more appropriate time.

By learning how to elicit and calibrate someone's state, we can gain the information necessary to enable us to respond more appropriately with our body and mind, and this in turn establishes a deeper level of understanding and rapport.

Anchors

Once a state has been elicited and calibrated, we then need to "anchor" it, so that we can access the desired state at will. An anchor is usually an external stimulus that, when triggered, provides a direct link to our desired physiological or mental state.

Any new behaviour that we learn begins by being linked to a stimulus. For example, the phone rings and you immediately feel the desire to pick it up.

Rookie Buster

Any new behaviour that we learn begins by being linked to a stimulus.

When we experience a strong emotion as a response to an experience, both the experience and its response will be linked and stored within the subconscious as a memory. These memories are known in NLP terms as "anchors".

Anchors are often created when a person experiences a situation that contains a high level of emotional content or when the experience is frequently repeated. An example of a powerful, negative anchored state is a phobia (such as a fear of public speaking, of spiders or of heights).

Anchors linked to our emotional states are very powerful and persuasive, and can provide us with a very influential tool to apply to our behaviour.

Tapping into and recreating our resourceful states using anchors provides us with a methodology that can help us manipulate our own and other people's behaviour. Anchors allow us to choose how we feel and how we wish to experience the events within our lives.

Anchors can be linked to any stimulus (fingers, words, feelings, people, places), but for personal use, it is often useful to link the trigger to a physical stimulus that can be easily accessed.

Coach's notes

Learning how to anchor the perfect resourceful state

1. Identify the particular resourceful state you want.
2. Now go back through your memories and remember a time when you have experienced that resource. Spend a couple of minutes reliving all the elements of this memory. (What did you see, hear, feel, what was your physiology like, how did you sound, etc.)
3. Break state.
4. Now choose a physical stimulus to which to anchor this state – for example, your finger.
5. Now put yourself fully back into that experience again, and spend a couple of minutes fully associating with all the submodalities (qualities) heightening the experience. When your emotions are at their peak, trigger your anchor (for example, squeeze your fingers) and hold this state for as long as you can, then break it.
6. Repeat Step 5, at least two more times.
7. Break state.
8. Now test your anchor. Fire your stimulus and notice your subconscious respond with your desired state.

Go for it! If you practise calibrating other people's states, you will quickly learn to notice whether or not your communication is having the desired affect. You cannot not communicate, and because of this it's important that you learn how to recognize the impact your communication is actually having upon your intended recipients.

By paying attention to another person's physiology, language and perceptions of their reality, you will always gain access to the information you need to enable your communication and subsequent influence to be constantly powerful and effective.

Notes

If we want to learn how to begin doing anything new, then we need to create a strategy for our subconscious mind to follow in order for us to reach our behavioural destination. In the same way that a company needs to have a business plan to highlight its objectives, so our sub-conscious needs a plan in order to deliver all of our ambitions and goals. In this chapter we are going to go through the basic process that will provide all the tools you need, so you can begin developing your own strategies in order to attain your goals and master all your ambitions.

CHAPTER 10

Preparing for the future

Strategies

Every single behaviour of ours has a strategy enabling it, a step-by-step process that guides our subconscious mind towards achieving our desired goal and outcomes. This basic strategy has been developed so you can apply it to any situation, goal or ambition: presentations, interviews, cold calling, appraisals, self employment, recruitment, management, training, confidence, business planning, etc.

Step 1: Know what your goal is

To create any new behaviour, your subconscious mind first needs a positive intent, the reason "why" behind your directional goal. What do *you* want? What do you want to achieve specifically? Your subconscious needs a target in order to know where to aim. (See the exercise in Chapter 2, "Creating our targets".)

158

Rookie Buster

To create any new behaviour, your subconscious mind first needs a positive intent.

Step 2: Beliefs and values

Is your goal congruent with your current values and beliefs? Why do you want this?

(See the exercise in Chapter 5, "Changing your values".)

What is stopping you from attaining it?

Exercise: Manipulating your beliefs

Our beliefs drive our behaviour, but can also limit it and get in the way of our goals. If you have always had a burning ambition to become your own boss and a desire to become self employed, what's actually stopping you?

- "I'm not lucky enough."
- "I haven't got the confidence I need."
- "I don't have the stamina to work for myself."

If you find the only thing standing in the way of you, your perfect career and your life is just your negative belief structure, then apply the exercise below and finally choose to change it. This is similar to the exercise in Chapter 5, but it reappears now in the broader context of the three steps described here. (You may find it easier to write down your responses on a piece of paper.)

1. Think of a positive belief you know to be true; for example, "I am a great salesman," "I'm incredibly organized," or "I'm a people person."

   (If you're struggling to find a belief, use something else you know is definitely true, such as "The world is round," "There are seven days in the week," "Water is wet," and so on.)

Now think clearly about this belief, acknowledge it and become aware of how your representational systems are recreating it within your mind.

Do you get a picture, have a feeling, or hear a sound? What are the submodalities of these sensory experiences?

How do you recognize this fact to be true? (For example, "I know it's true, because I have a strong feeling about it.")

2. Now think of the belief that is holding you back and you would like to change; for example, "I'm not a confident salesman," or "I'm not dynamic enough to run my own business."

3. Change the language structure of your negative belief into its positive counterpart (the thing you want to achieve). For example, "I'm a confident salesman," "I am dynamic and I can run my own business."

4. Now become aware once more of all the submodalities of the belief you know to be true, the feelings you get, the pictures you see, all of your sensory acknowledgements and representations of this belief.

5. Now superimpose all the positive qualities from the belief you know to be true on to the new belief you would like to create.

6. Repeat stages 4 and 5 over and over until this statement contains all the submodality qualities necessary for you now to believe this Belief statement to be true (instead of your original negative belief).

Step 3: Overcoming obstacles

Often when we are attempting to access our goals we come across obstacles that get in our way.

160   Fear

Fear is a common obstacle that faces everyone at some point or another. Instinctively its creation is a positive, and it actually provides us with the protection we need in order to function safely throughout our everyday life. However it can also sometimes become misguided in its behavioural direction, and can steer our behaviour away from achieving things we actually may want or need to experience. (Presentations, cold calling, sales, interviews, heights, lifts, spiders, etc.)

Most of our fears are originally created because of a negatively anchored response to a trigger contained within a previous experience or memory.

The fast phobia cure

This cure teaches us how to disassociate from our memories and their negative influence.

1. Identify your phobic response or the unpleasant experience that you wish to overcome.

2. Now imagine you are sitting in a cinema, looking up at the big screen, and being projected onto this screen is a movie detailing your experience of your phobia. (Disassociation.) It is important for you to remember that you are safe before and after the unpleasant experience.

3. Now imagine yourself floating out of the you that is sitting in the cinema seat looking up at the screen, and move yourself a couple of rows back in the cinema, so you are now looking at yourself, watching you, experiencing your phobia on the cinema screen.

4. Now repeat this process again, except this time float out of the you that is sitting a couple of rows back and imagine you are now standing in the projection booth, looking down on yourself a couple of rows back, looking at yourself looking up at the cinema screen.

5. Now imagine that whilst you can see yourself in the projection booth watching yourself in the seats, watching the film of you on

the screen, you press a button in the projection booth, that re-runs the movie right back to the beginning, back to the time before your negative experience began, back to a time when you were safe.

6. Now imagine the movie has been turned to black and white. Begin running the movie through, starting before your negative experience began, through until after the experience had finished and you were once again safe.

7. Now imagine the screen shrinking right down in size, so it becomes the size of a small portable TV, and then imagine the picture on the screen completely disappearing, turning the screen completely white, the image gone.

8. Float back out of the projection booth, out of both seats and into the end of your film.

9. Now imagine running the film backwards, in full colour, really quickly. As if you're experiencing the whole film in reverse. As you do this, imagine the theme tune to a really silly cartoon, or circus music (it doesn't matter what, as long as it makes you laugh). If you struggle to imagine music, then do this exercise whilst actually listening to some really silly upbeat tune. Run your phobic movie right back to the beginning, experiencing everything again in reverse, right back to the beginning when you were safe.

10. Repeat steps 8 and 9 through again until you find that you are now comfortable with the experience.

11. Now imagine going into the future and finding yourself in a situation which would be likely to prompt the phobic response. If you find you have any traces of discomfort, repeat the exercise again.

Understanding there is no such thing as failure, only feedback

Your mind is always learning, but will generally have to go through a process of trial and error before it reaches a stage of unconscious competence (see Chapter 1) and produces the results you actually desire.

Unfortunately as we get older, we allow our fear of failure to influence our desire to learn, and because of this we often give up and quit before we manage to master a desired new skill. This means that we often end up missing out on the various new opportunities to learn, instead of accepting failure for what it really is, an option on the natural learning curve.

Rookie Buster

As we get older, we allow our fear of failure to influence our desire to learn.

When you are attempting to learn any new skill, ask yourself:

- What am I aiming to achieve?
- What have I achieved so far?
- What feedback have I had?
- What lessons have I learned?
- How can I put them to positive use?
- How will I measure success?

The next time you find yourself frustrated and struggling, run through the above questions, pick yourself up and have another go. Practice makes perfect.

Tackling the objections of others

Sometimes, despite all of our best intentions, we can still find ourselves occasionally clashing with others. This can be because of a difference of opinion, a misinterpretation of ideas or a simple lack of common understanding and grounding. Conflict is very common in business, but it can also arise within in any situation that involves communicating with others. Remember, everyone views the world from different perspectives, and no two realities are the same.

Rookie Buster

Everyone views the world from different perspectives, and no two realities are the same.

A talented therapist, Robert Dilts, created an NLP model that allows us to explore relationships further, providing us with a tool that provides insight into another person's reality and perceptions upon a situation.

The Meta mirror
The Meta mirror will help you to prepare for many possible scenarios you may face:
- Conflict between staff.
- Interviews.
- Relationship management.

1. First choose a relationship you wish to explore.
2. Now imagine three positions on the ground in front of you (you can draw circles, place a marker on the floor or just use your imagination).

1.

2. **3.**

3. Stand in position 1 (this is your point of view). Imagine that you are looking at the other person in position 2. Ask yourself, what am I experiencing, thinking and feeling as I'm looking at the other person?

164

4. Step out of position 1, break state and then go and stand at position 2 (this is the other person's point of view). Imagine now that you're standing within the other person looking back at yourself in first position. Ask yourself, "What are they experiencing, thinking and feeling as they look at me?"

5. Now step out of that position, break state and step into position 3 (the independent observer). Imagine looking at both people in this relationship impartially. Look at yourself in position 1 and at the person in position 2. What's your opinion from here?

6. Break state and then go back and revisit position 2. Ask yourself, how is this opinion different now? What, if anything, has changed?

7. Finish by coming back to position 1 again. Ask yourself, how is this position different now? What if anything, has changed?

Step 4: Create the required state

Our states can be mental, emotional or physical, and they have a massive influence over our ability to perform certain tasks. If we want to achieve any particular objective, it is of paramount importance that our states are congruent with our objectives.

Rookie Buster

If we want to achieve any particular objective, it is of paramount importance that our states are congruent with our objectives.

Once you have worked out Step 1 (Know what your goal is), spend a couple of moments thinking about what state(s) you are going to need to be in for this to be achieved.

Example

Presentation: Focused, confident, motivated and vibrant.
Interview: Focused, confident, relaxed and quick thinking.
Managing: Confident, strong, happy and organized.

Exercise: Creating states – motivation

You can switch motivation for confidence or any other state that you wish to recreate. You need to choose two anchors for this exercise. (See "Anchors" in Chapter 9.)

1. Think back to a time when you were really motivated to learn, do or start something. (Choose something that you found easy to do and that you really enjoyed learning, something almost unnatural for you not to know how to do now.)
2. Remember all the submodalities of this memory. What do you hear, see and feel?
3. Make all your images bright and strong, make any internal/ external sounds supportive and strong, intensify your feelings and truly breathe all the elements of this memory in.
4. Once you've built this memory up to an optimum level and you can feel it peaking, anchor it to your chosen Anchor 1.
5. Repeat this step three times, until you feel you have created a really strong anchor.
6. Now remember how confident and fantastic you felt once you knew you had learned this new thing and you could do it easily, subconsciously, as though it was the most natural thing in the world.
7. Remember all the submodalities of this memory. What do you hear, see and feel?
8. Make all your images bright and strong, make any internal/

external sounds supportive and strong, intensify your feelings and truly breathe all the elements of this memory in.

9. Once you've built this memory up to an optimum level and you can feel it peaking, anchor it to your chosen Anchor 2.
10. Repeat this step three times, until you feel you have created a really strong anchor.
11. Now think of the new thing you want to be motivated into obtaining, achieving or doing.
12. Imagine the processes, and run the memory through from the beginning to the middle and right through to the end. Imagine all the submodalities involved. What do you hear, see and feel?
13. Once you have this process clear, run it through your mind again, whilst firing off anchor 1 at the same time.
14. Repeat step 13 three times.
15. Now repeat step 13 but whilst firing off anchor 2 instead.
16. Repeat step 15 three times.
17. Repeat step 15 but fire off both anchors at the same time. Imagine the motivation and anticipation for wanting to learn something and the fantastic feeling of achievement and subconscious knowing, once you have achieved it.
18. Repeat step 17 three times, test and then future pace on to future situations (see below).

Step 5: The attainment of dreams

Once you have worked out your goals, re-evaluated your values and beliefs, overcome any objections and created the required states, the only step left for you to take is that of action.

You have to choose to turn your aspirations into reality.

If you want to become a successful billionaire, a top sales person or simply motivate your staff into action, then you must choose to actively begin implementing and practising all of the understanding you have now gained.

Simply reading this book is not enough!

Where do you want your future to lead, and have you pre-pro-   167
grammed your mental diary with the appropriate appointments to
take you there?

Future pacing

The subconscious mind has no analytical thought, and every action it
performs is a result of pre-programming and expectation, past, present
and future.

So what is your subconscious business plan for the future, and is it
mapped out on your time line?

1. Spend a couple of moments thinking about your goal. Imagine
   every single tiny detail of it, all of the submodalities involved, how
   you will feel, what you will see and what you will hear. How will
   you know when you have achieved it and what will it mean to
   you?
2. Create the imagination strongly within your mind and hold it
   there for a couple of minutes, enjoying the daydream that is your
   perfect reality.
3. Break state.
4. Now imagine your time line running with your past either behind
   or to the left of you (depending upon which feels the most
   natural), through yourself right now (the present)
   and out in front of you or to the right, heading
   off into your future.
5. Now imagine floating out of yourself in
   the present and heading off into your
   future to the time when your goal has
   been attained.
6. Imagine standing in your future,
   experiencing the success of your
   achievement, knowing all the steps you
   have taken to lead you here.
7. Now imagine going further down your time
   line, one year from now, five years, ten years,

and imagine how your life will be as you continue aspiring towards the future of your dreams.

8. Spend a couple of moments daydreaming every element of this new life clearly. Truly etch out every detail upon your subconscious diary.

9. Now imagine floating up above your time line so that you are able to look down at its entirety.

10. Become aware of all the steps you have created and taken that have led you towards your future goals. Spend a couple of moments conjuring all the details necessary to appear on your subconscious business plan, your blueprint, your mental diary, both present and future.

11. When you feel you have created and understood all the details required to lead your subconscious to your perfect future, imagine floating back down into the moment of your original goal's attainment. Associate with the experience once more.

12. Now step back into yourself in the present, and imagine yourself looking out on to your brilliant future and become aware of a sensation of excitement, possibility, motivation and ambition to begin stepping on to the path of your amazing life.

Coach's notes  169

Putting it into practice

Work through and follow all of the steps in Chapter 10, or, if you prefer, to start with simply choose the NLP exercise that is the most appropriate for you and your situation at present.

All of the exercises in this book have been written for you to use as a guide, a manual to highlight to your mind a different way of maybe approaching the world around you, providing you with options and opportunity, so you can choose how you want to interpret information, respond to others, influence your colleagues or simply learn how to understand and manipulate the influence you have upon yourself.

As with any new subject, you cannot expect to pick up this book, read it once and then suddenly find yourself with all of the answers and solutions in one magic wave of the wand. It will take time, commitment and, most importantly, practice!

Some of the exercises in this book will provide you with instantaneous results, others may take a little more time, feedback, adjustment and learning.

However, luckily for you, the process of learning is already something you are instinctively brilliant at. After all, once upon a time you learned to walk and speak a new language, and maybe you have learned to drive a car or play a new sport.

There was a time in your life when you were consciously incompetent at one thing or another, but through practice, motivation, patience and time, you have learned to become better and more skilled, and are now (probably unconsciously) very competent at whatever it is.

You can learn to become anything you want to in life. The ultimate question is: What do you choose?

Go for it! The fantastic thing about NLP is that there is no right or wrong, but there is always a choice. In business you can use NLP to learn skills, overcome your obstacles and conflicts, and influence your colleagues, clients and staff. Most importantly, NLP provides you with a methodology that gives you the ability and the freedom to choose how you wish to perceive and respond to your environment, both internally and externally. Life can be everything you want it to be – so what do you choose and how are you going to go about turning your dreams into your reality?

Appendix

Additional exercise

Collapsing negative anchors

1. Imagine two circles on the floor in front of you. Make one a positive circle and the other negative.
2. Step into the negative circle and think of a negative memory or experience.
3. Spend a couple of moments recalling all the details of it (submodalities). Recall everything that happened and how it made you feel.
4. Break state.
5. Step into the positive circle and think of a really positive experience, one that makes you feel truly fantastic and happy. Spend a couple of minutes truly associating with this experience. Strengthen all the submodalities within this positive experience so that it feels stronger than the negative experience did.
6. While you are standing within the positive circle, begin trying to think about the negative feeling. Maybe even talk out loud about

172   it and as you do, notice how the negative feelings and your
       physiology attached to this emotion have now changed.
  7.   Step out of the circle and break state.
  8.   Now step back into the positive circle again and repeat steps 5 and
       6. Notice that the more you attempt to think about your negative
       experience, the more difficult it becomes to recall the negative
       elements of it.
  9.   Repeat and practise.

Glossary

Accessing cues
Subtle behavioural traits, responses that indicate which representational systems are being operated. Can be eye movements, body
posture, gestures, tonality, etc.

Anchors
Can be set up either intentionally or naturally. The process by which
an external stimulus can trigger an internal automatic response.
Response is often a physiological sensation – fear, happiness, etc.

Auditory
To do with the sense of hearing.

Associate
Experiencing something from your own perspective, as if you have
stepped into the experiencing – seeing what you see, hearing the
sounds you hear and feeling what you're feeling inside yourself.

Behaviour
Our specific activity by which we interact with our environment both
internally and externally.

Beliefs

Generalizations that you hold about the world, which are closely knitted to the values you hold. Beliefs can be empowering or limiting, and they can tint the way that you see the world. The beliefs that you have about something are not always correct, and this applies to beliefs about yourself and others.

Calibration

A skill which involves being able to tune into another person's feelings and the state they are experiencing by applying knowledge of body language and non-verbal signs which could indicate different feelings.

Chunking

The organization of information into smaller or larger pieces to present information on a logical level, in relevance to the information being processed and the person processing it. "Chunking down" means becoming more specific; tiny details. "Chunking up" means dealing with information on a larger, sometimes more abstract level; the bigger picture.

Congruence

When a person's internal strategies, beliefs, values and behaviours are all in alignment, unified and in agreement, working together for the same outcome.

Conscious mind

The mind that you're consciously aware with as you read this. The conscious mind is in charge of your thoughts in the present moment, and can hold around seven chunks of information (plus or minus two) before it gets overloaded. You also use your conscious mind to keep aware of your environment at each moment, and to make decisions with.

174 **Deep structure**
Our internal neurological maps that we use to interpret our own perceived reality of our environment.

Deletion
Involves deleting the details from what you are experiencing. This can
happen in everyday language, when you can either get the specific
details through using the Meta model to help understanding of the
situation, or use general language to help elicit change by using it in
Milton model language patterns.

Distortion
The process by which information is altered or changed to inaccu-
rately represent itself within someone's personal reality. Often related
to an individual's belief system.

Disassociate
Looking in on a certain experience as an observer, such as when you
watch a movie.

Ecology check
Making sure that the outcome a client is aiming towards fits with the
different parts of their life to make the change stick.

Elicitation
The gathering of information from oneself or from another, either
through direct or indirect observation or questioning.

Environment
The surrounding, external world, context or situation in which we
exist, with which we interact and to which we respond.

Eye accessing cues
Certain eye movements that signal which representational system
(visual, auditory or kinaesthetic) someone is using at any moment.

Future pacing

Rehearsing future situations, experiences and outcomes in order to prepare the subconscious mind, so that it has a chance to practise the desired behavioural responses.

Generalization

This occurs when you generalize one learning experience to all future similar experiences. For example, if one presentation doesn't go the way you plan, you may generalize this learning to other presentations. Generalization can be detected in language, both in Meta model and Milton model patterns. Generalizations usually include words such as always, never and can't.

Gustatory

To do with the sense of taste.

Hypnosis

A common natural trance-like state that you experience on a daily basis. During hypnosis your conscious mind relaxes while your unconscious mind is active, and becomes able to absorb suggestions it agrees with to allow positive change.

Installation

The learning and creation of a new behaviour, strategy or response. Can be done through reframing, future pacing, anchoring or metaphors.

Kinaesthetic

To do with the sense of feeling, both emotional and tactile.

Leading

This is the stage that can occur in rapport after you have paced someone else's view of the world. Leading involves bringing another person around to what you want to happen in a certain situation.

176 **Matching and mirroring**
A way of building rapport with others by matching their view of the world as they see it, from their map. This involves allowing yourself to be influenced by their beliefs about the world and also mirroring their body language, including body movements and other non-verbal signals such as voice tone and speed of speech.

Meta model
A model containing language patterns which allow us to break down another person's language (or what you say to yourself) to recover the real meaning or deep structure. This model includes patterns of generalization, distortion and deletion.

Meta programs
Deeply held values that we are not always aware of and that direct our behaviour and motivations. Various Meta programs can run at alternate faces of our lives and independently or simultaneously. Meta programs include towards/away from, global/detail, sameness/difference and thought/feeling.

Metaphor
The explanation of a subject, experience or situation using a process of thinking that links understanding one thing to the terms of another, i.e. by stories, analogies or tales.

Milton model
An NLP term used to describe the methodology behind Milton Erickson's methods. The Milton model uses generalized language, including distortion, generalization and deletion, which allows the listener to choose their own more suitable interpretation. The general language used in the Milton model helps the listener to access their own unconscious resources and facilitates change.

Modelling
The process of observing, mapping, copying and reproducing another's behaviour.

Olfactory
To do with the sense of smell.

Outcomes
Our goals, desired states, ambitions and aspirations for the future.

Pacing
A method used in rapport building to establish subconscious communication before installing or introducing a change of conversation, idea, concept or behaviour.

Parts
A metaphorical way of describing the various elements or structures in place in our subconscious.

Perceptual positions
This NLP technique involves looking at a situation from several different angles including your own point of view, another person's view and as an outside observer of a problem. Provides different insights into a problem and helps to produce a solution and empathy, and facilitate the building of rapport.

Predicates
Process words used to describe a person's thought process when using language to represent their reality, thinking and understanding via their representational systems.

Presuppositions
Statements that are taken for granted in order to make sense of a communicated sentence.

Rapport
Occurs when you build up respectful trust with others. Essential to effective communication. It is also a pillar of NLP.

RAS (reticular activating system)
A nifty system in your mind which helps you to filter the vast amount of information that reaches your senses every second so that you don't get overloaded. The only information this system allows past its barriers is information that is survival crucial, new and fresh, and highly emotional in its content. Additionally it helps you to block out from your awareness anything that isn't important to you in the moment.

Reframing
Looking at a situation in a different way to change the meaning it has for you. For example, if you want to feel more confident, by acting as if you are a confident individual you can see the world and challenging situations in a different way.

Representational systems
Representational systems include your senses, which pick up information from the outside world. They include visual, kinaesthetic, auditory, gustatory and olfactory systems.

State
Is the result of what we think and feel internally, and the physical sensations which follow from these.

Strategy
Behavioural processes; steps used to achieve a specific goal, process or outcome.

Submodalities
The specific elements (qualities) to our internal representational thinking. Sounds, shapes, focus, feelings, size, depths, etc.

Swish
An NLP process used to replace an unwanted state/behaviour with a more desirable state/behaviour.

Third position
Choosing to experience reality from another individual's perspective
or point of view.

Time line
Our personal mental diary, in which we store our memories, experiences, predictions and images for the past, present and future.

TOTE model
Stands for Test, Operate, Test, Exit. This model helps to detect how you
and others use your submodalities to reach a certain goal. This allows
you to change the submodalities that aren't working for you in order
to help you achieve your goals, and also to help others with theirs.

Translating
Rephrasing a word or sentence in a way that the listener can interpret
and understand.

Trance
A heightened state of internal focus and attention, usually upon few
stimuli.

Unconscious mind
Your unconscious mind is in charge of the processes outside your
awareness. These include creating and storing memories. The unconscious mind helps to keep your body functions going (such as the
beating of your heart) and is also thirsty for new learning experiences
and is very creative. Your unconscious also helps you exercise your
moral beliefs.

VAK
Shorthand for three of the representational systems: visual, auditory
and kinaesthetic.

180 **Values**
Values are things in your life that are important to you and that you choose to live by. For example, your values could include money, recognition, health, friends or family. To be able to live your values there needs to be a trade-off, as you cannot live them all at once.

Visual
To do with the sense of sight.

Well-formedness/conditions
The specific information detailing a goal and the steps needed in order to achieve it, taking into consideration all the individual's motivations, resources, environment, beliefs, feedback, contexts and sensory awareness.

References

Andreas, S., and C. Faulkner, *NLP: The new technology of achievement*, Nicholas Brealey Publishing, London, 2002.

Bandler, R., and J. Grinder, *Frogs into Princes: Neuro-linguistic Programming*, Real People Press, Boulder, Colorado, 1979.

Bandler, R., P. McKenna and M. Neill, *Neuro-linguistic Programming: NLP Master Practitioner Manual*, NLP Seminars Group International, UK, 1996.

McDermott, I., and W. Jago, *The NLP coach: A comprehensive guide to personal wellbeing and professional success*, Judy Piatkus Limited, London, 2001.

Molden, D., and P. Hutchinson, *Brilliant NLP: What the most successful people know, do and say*, Pearson Education Limited, Harlow, 2008.

O'Connor, J., *NLP Workbook: A practical guide to achieving the results you want*, Element, London, 2001.

O'Connor, J., and J. Seymour, *Introducing NLP: Psychological skills for understanding and influencing people*, Thorsons, London, 1993.

Owen, N., *The magic of metaphor*, Crown House Publishing, Carmarthen, 2001.

Ready, R., and K. Burton, *Neuro-linguistic Programming for Dummies*, John Wiley & Sons Ltd., Chichester, 2004.

Index